SHAKESPEARE

MACBETH

NOTES

COLES EDITORIAL BOARD

Bound to stay open

Publisher's Note

Otabind (Ota-bind). This book has been bound using the patented Otabind process. You can open this book at any page, gently run your finger down the spine, and the pages will lie flat.

ABOUT COLES NOTES

COLES NOTES have been an indispensible aid to students on five continents since 1948.

COLES NOTES are available for a wide range of individual literary works. Clear, concise explanations and insights are provided along with interesting interpretations and evaluations.

Proper use of COLES NOTES will allow the student to pay greater attention to lectures and spend less time taking notes. This will result in a broader understanding of the work being studied and will free the student for increased participation in discussions.

COLES NOTES are an invaluable aid for review and exam preparation as well as an invitation to explore different interpretive paths.

COLES NOTES are written by experts in their fields. It should be noted that any literary judgement expressed herein is just that – the judgement of one school of thought. Interpretations that diverge from, or totally disagree with any criticism may be equally valid.

COLES NOTES are designed to supplement the text and are not intended as a substitute for reading the text itself. Use of the NOTES will serve not only to clarify the work being studied, but should enhance the readers enjoyment of the topic.

ISBN 0-7740-3211-1

© COPYRIGHT 2000 AND PUBLISHED BY
COLES PUBLISHING COMPANY
TORONTO - CANADA
PRINTED IN CANADA

Manufactured by Webcom Limited
Cover finish: Webcom's Exclusive **DURACOAT**

CONTENTS

Character Sketches

WILLIAM SHAKESPEARE
LIFE AND WORKS
Biographical Sketch

With the epithet "Dear Son of Memory", Milton praised Shakespeare as one constantly in our memories and brother of the Muses. Certainly no other author has held such sway over the literary world, undiminished through some three and a half centuries of shifting artistic tastes. Shakespeare's plots and his characters have continued to be a living reality for us; as his well known contemporary Ben Jonson wrote, in a familiar tribute, "Thou . . . art alive still, while thy Booke doth live,/ And we have wits to read, and praise to give."

The Early Years

Despite such acclaim and the scholarship it has spawned, our knowledge of Shakespeare's life is sketchy, filled with more questions than answers, even after we prune away the misinformation accumulated over the years. He was baptized on April 26, 1564, in Holy Trinity Church, Stratford-on-Avon. As it was customary to baptize children a few days after birth, we conjecture that he was born on April 23. The monument erected in Stratford states that he died on April 23, 1616, in his fifty-third year.

William was the third child of John Shakespeare, who came to Stratford from Snitterfield before 1532 as a "whyttawer" (tanner) and glover, and Mary Arden, daughter of a wealthy "gentleman of worship" from Wilmecote. They married around 1557. Since John Shakespeare owned one house on Greenhill Street and two on Henley Street, we cannot be certain where William was born, though the Henley Street shrine draws many tourists each year. William's two older sisters died in infancy, but three brothers and two other sisters survived at least into childhood.

Shakespeare's father was fairly well-to-do, dealing in farm products and wool, and owning considerable property in Stratford. After holding a series of minor municipal offices he was elected alderman in 1565, high bailiff (roughly similar to the mayor of today) in 1568, and chief alderman in 1571. There are no records of young Will Shakespeare's education (though there are many unfounded legends), but he undoubtedly attended the town school maintained by the burgesses, which prepared its students for the universities. Ben Jonson's line about Shakespeare's having "small *Latine*, and lesse *Greeke*" refers not to his education but to his lack of indebtedness to the classical writers and dramatists.

On November 27, 1582, a licence to marry was issued to "Willelmum Shaxpere *et* Annam Whateley *de* Temple Grafton," and on

1

the next day a marriage bond for "Willm Shagspere" and "Anne Hathwey of Stratford" was signed by Fulk Sandells and John Richardson, farmers of Stratford. This bond stated that there was no "lawful let or impediment by reason of any precontract, consanguinity, affinity, or by any other lawful means whatsoever"; thus "William and Anne (were) to be married together with once asking of the banns of matrimony." The problem of Anne Whateley has led many researchers and some detractors to argue all kinds of improbabilities, such as the existence of two different Shakespeares and the forging of documents to conceal Shakespeare's true identity. The actual explanation seems to be simple: the clerk who made the marriage licence entry apparently copied the name "Whateley" from a preceding entry, as a glance at the full sheet suggests. (Incidentally, Nicholas Rowe in his life of Shakespeare, published in 1709, well before the discovery of these marriage records, gave Anne's name as Hathaway.) The problems of marriage with Anne Hathaway — he was eighteen and she was twenty-six — and of the bond have caused similar consternation. Why did these two marry when there was such a discrepancy of age? Why only one saying of the banns (rather than the usual three)? Why the emphasis on a possible legal impediment? The answer here is not simple or definite, but the birth of a daughter Susanna, baptized at Holy Trinity on May 26, 1583, seems to explain the odd circumstances. It should be recognized, however, that an engagement to marry was considered legally binding in those days (we still have breach-of-promise suits today) and that premarital relations were not unusual or frowned upon when an engagement had taken place. The circumstances already mentioned, Shakespeare's ensuing activities, and his will bequeathing to Anne "my second best bed with the furniture" have suggested to some that their marriage was not entirely happy. Their other children, the twins Hamnet and Judith, were christened on February 2, 1585.

Theatrical Life

Shakespeare's years before and immediately after the time of his marriage are not charted, but rumor has him as an apprentice to a master butcher or as a country teacher or an actor with some provincial company. He is supposed to have run away from whatever he was doing for livelihood and to have gone to London, where he soon attached himself to some theatrical group. At this time there were only two professional houses established in the London environs, The Theatre (opened in 1576) and The Curtain (opened in 1577). His first connection with the theater was reputedly as holder of horses; that is, one of the stage crew, but a most inferior assignment. Thereafter he became an actor (perhaps at this time he met Ben Jonson), a writer, and a director. Such experience had its mark in the theatricality of his plays. We do know that he was established in London by 1592, when Robert Greene lamented in *A Groatsworth of Wit* (September, 1592) that professional actors had gained priority in the theater over university-trained writers like himself: "There is an upstart Crow, beautified with our feathers, that with his *Tygers hart wrapt in a Players hyde*, supposes he is as well able to bombast out a lanke verse as the best of you: and beeing an absolute *Iohannes fac totum* (Jack-of-all-trades), is in his owne conceit the onely Shake-scene in a countrey." An apology for Greene's ill-humored statement by Henry Chettle, the editor of the pamphlet, appeared around December 1592 in *Kind-Hart's Dream*.

Family Affairs

To return to the known details of family life, Shakespeare's son Hamnet was buried at Stratford on August 11, 1596; his father was given a coat of arms on October 20, 1596; and he purchased New Place (a refurbished tourist attraction today) on May 4, 1597. The London playwright obviously had not severed connections with his birthplace, and he was reflecting his new affluence by being known as William Shakespeare of Stratford-upon-Avon, in the County of Warwick, Gentleman. His father was buried in Stratford on September 8, 1601; his mother, on September 9, 1608. His daughter Susanna married Dr. John Hall on June 5, 1607, and they had a child named Elizabeth. His other daughter, Judith, married Thomas Quiney on February 10, 1616, without special licence, during Lent and was thus excommunicated. Shakespeare revised his will on March 25, 1616, and was buried on April 25, 1616 (according to the parish register). A monument by Gerard Janssen was erected in the Holy Trinity chancel in 1623 but many, like Milton several years later, protested:

> What needs my *Shakespeare* for his honour'd Bones,
> The labour of an age in piled Stone, . . .
> Thou in our wonder and astonishment
> Hast built thy self a live-long Monument.

Shakespeare's Writings

Order of Appearance

Dating of Shakespeare's early plays, while based on inconclusive evidence, has tended to hover around the early 1590's. Almost certainly it is his chronicles of Henry the Sixth that Philip Henslowe, an important theatrical manager of the day, referred to in his diary as being performed during March-May, 1592. An allusion to these plays also occurs in Thomas Nashe's *Piers Penniless His Supplication to the Devil* (August, 1592). Greene's quotation about a tiger is a paraphrase of "O tiger's heart wrapt in a woman's hide" from *Henry VI*, Part III.

The first published work to come from Shakespeare's hand was *Venus and Adonis* (1593), a long stanzaic poem, dedicated to Henry

3

Wriothesley, Earl of Southampton. A year later *The Rape of Lucrece* appeared, also dedicated to Southampton. Perhaps poetry was pursued during these years because the London theaters were closed as a result of a virulent siege of plague. The *Sonnets*, published in 1609, may owe something to Southampton, who had become Shakespeare's patron. Perhaps some were written as early as the first few years of the 1590's. They were mentioned (along with a number of plays) in 1598 by Francis Meres in his *Palladis Tamia*, and sonnets 138 and 144 were printed without authority by William Jaggard in *The Passionate Pilgrim* (1599).

There is a record of a performance of *A Comedy of Errors* at Gray's Inn (one of the law colleges) on December 28, 1594, and, during early 1595, Shakespeare was paid, along with the famous actors Richard Burbage and William Kempe, for performances before the Queen by the Lord Chamberlain's Men, a theatrical company formed the year before. The company founded the Globe Theatre on the south side of the Thames in 1599 and became the King's Men when James ascended the throne. Records show frequent payments to the company through its general manager John Heminge. From 1595 through 1614 there are numerous references to real estate transactions and other legal matters, to many performances, and to various publications connected with Shakespeare.

Order of Publication

The first plays to be printed were *Titus Andronicus* around February, 1594, and the garbled versions of *Henry VI*, Parts II and III in 1594. (Some scholars, however, question whether the last two are versions of *Henry VI*, Parts II and III, and some dispute Shakespeare's authorship.) Thereafter *Richard III* appeared in 1597 and 1598; *Richard II*, in 1597 and twice in 1598; *Romeo and Juliet*, in 1597 (a pirated edition) and 1599, and many others. Some of the plays appear in individual editions, with or without Shakespeare's name on the title page,but eighteen are known only from their appearance in the first collected volume (the so-called First Folio) of 1623. The editors were Heminge and Henry Condell, another member of Shakespeare's company. *Pericles* was omitted from the First Folio although it had appeared in 1609, 1611, and 1619; it was added to the Third Folio in 1664.

There was reluctance to publish plays at this time for various reasons; many plays were carelessly written for fast production; collaboration was frequent; plays were not really considered *reading* matter; they were sometimes circulated in manuscript; and the theatrical company, not the author, owned the rights. Those plays given individual publication appeared in a quarto, so named from the size of the page. A single sheet of paper was folded twice to make four leaves (thus *quarto*) or eight pages; these four leaves constitute one signature (one section of a bound book). A page measures about 6¾ in. x 8½ in. On the other hand, a folio sheet is folded once to make two leaves or four pages; three sheets, or twelve pages, constitute a signature. The page is approximately 8½ in. x 13⅜ in.

Authorized publication occurred when a company disbanded, when money was needed but rights were to be retained, when a play failed or ran into licensing difficulties (thus, hopefully, the printed work would justify the play against the criticism), or when a play had been pirated. Authorized editions are called good quartos. Piratical publication might occur when the manuscript of a play had circulated privately, when a member of a company desired money for himself, or when a stenographer or memorizer took the play down in the theater (such a version was recognizable by inclusion of stage directions derived from an eyewitness, by garbled sections, etc.). Pirated editions are called bad quartos; there are at least five bad quartos of Shakespeare's plays.

Authenticity of Works

Usually thirty-seven plays are printed in modern collections of Shakespeare's works but some recent scholars have urged the addition of two more: *Edward III* and *Two Noble Kinsmen*. A case has also been advanced, unconvincingly, for a fragment of the play on Sir Thomas More. At times, six of the generally-accepted plays have been questioned: *Henry VI*, Parts I, II and III, *Timon of Athens*, *Pericles* and *Henry VIII*. The first four are usually accepted today (one hopes all question concerning *Timon* has finally ended), but if Shakespeare did not write these plays in their entirety, he certainly wrote parts of them. Of course, collaboration in those days was commonplace. Aside from the two long narrative poems already mentioned and the sonnets (Nos. 1-152, but not Nos. 153-154), Shakespeare's poetic output is uncertain. *The Passionate Pilgrim* (1599) contains only five authenticated poems (two sonnets and three verses from *Love's Labour's Lost*); *The Phoenix and the Turtle* (1601) may be his, but the authenticity of *A Lover's Complaint* (appended to the sonnets) is highly questionable.

Who Was Shakespeare?

At this point we might mention a problem that has plagued Shakespeare study for over a century: who was Shakespeare? Those who would like to make the author of the plays someone else — Francis Bacon or the Earl of Oxford or even Christopher Marlowe (dead long before most of the plays were written) — have used the lack of information of Shakespeare's early years and the confusion in the evidence we have been examining to advance their candidate. But the major arguments against Shakespeare show the source of these speculators' disbelief to be in classconscious snobbery and perhaps in a perverse adherence to minority opinion. The most common argument is that no one of Shakespeare's background, lack of education, and lack of aristocratic experience could know all that the author knew. But study will reveal that such information was readily available in various popular sources, that some of it lies in the literary sources used for the play, and that Shakespeare was probably not totally lacking in education or in social decorum. The more significant question of style and tone is not dealt with — nor could it successfully be raised. Bacon, for example, no matter how much we admire his mind and his writings, exhibits a writing style diametrically opposite to Shakespeare's, a style most unpoetic and often flat. The student would be wise not to waste time rehashing these unfounded theories. No such question was raised in the seventeenth or eighteenth centuries, and no serious student of the plays today doubts that Shakespeare *was* Shakespeare.

Shakespeare's Plays

Exact dates for Shakespeare's plays remain a source of debate among scholars. The following serve only as a general frame of reference.

	COMEDIES	TRAGEDIES	HISTORIES
1591			Henry VI, Part I
1592	Comedy of Errors		Henry VI, Part II
1592	Two Gentlemen of Verona		Henry VI, Part III
1593	Love's Labour's Lost	Titus Andronicus	Richard III
1594			King John
1595	Midsummer Night's Dream	Romeo and Juliet	Richard II
1596	Merchant of Venice		
1596	Taming of the Shrew		
1597			Henry IV, Part I
1598	Much Ado About Nothing		Henry IV, Part II
1599	As You Like It	Julius Caesar	
1599	Merry Wives of Windsor		Henry V
1601	Twelfth Night	Hamlet	
1602	Troilus and Cressida		
1602	All's Well That Ends Well		
1604	Measure for Measure	Othello	
1605		King Lear	
1606		Macbeth	
1607		Timon of Athens	
1607		Antony and Cleopatra	
1608	Pericles		
1609		Coriolanus	
1610	Cymbeline		
1611	Winter's Tale		
1611	Tempest		
1613			Henry VIII

Shakespeare's England

The world of Elizabethan and Jacobean England was a world of growth and change. The great increase in the middle class, and in the population as a whole, demanded a new economy and means of livelihood, a new instrument of government (one recognizing "rights" and changed class structure), a new social code and a broad base of entertainment. The invention of printing a century before had contributed to that broader base, but it was the theater that supplied the more immediate needs of the greatest numbers. The theater grew and along with it came less-educated, more money-conscious writers, who gave the people what they wanted: entertainment. But Shakespeare, having passed through a brief period of hack writing, proceeded to set down important ideas in memorable language throughout most of his career. His plays, particularly the later ones, have been analyzed by recent critics in terms of literary quality through their metaphor, verse-line, relationships with psychology and myth, and elaborate structure. Yet Shakespeare was a man of the stage, and the plays were written to be performed. Only this will fully account for the humor of a deadly serious play like *Hamlet* or the spectacle of a *Coriolanus*.

Life in London

During Shakespeare's early years there, London was a walled city of about 200,000, with seven gates providing access to the city from the east, north, and west. It was geographically small and crisscrossed by narrow little streets and lanes. The various wards each had a parish church that dominated the life of the close-knit community. To the south and outside were slums and the haunts of criminal types, and farther out were the agricultural lands and huge estates. As the population increased and the central area declined, the fashionable people of the city moved toward the west, where the palace of Westminster lay. Houses were generally rented out floor by floor and sometimes room by room. Slums were common within the city, too, though close to pleasant enough streets and squares. "Merrie Olde England" was not really clean, nor were its people, for in those days there were no sewers or drains except the gutter in the middle of the street, into which garbage would be emptied to be floated off by the rain to Fleet ditch or Moor ditch. Plague was particularly ravaging in 1592, 1593-94 (when the theaters were closed to avoid contamination) and 1603. Medical knowledge, of course, was slight; ills were "cured" by amputation, leeching, blood-letting and cathartics. The city was (and still is) dominated by St. Paul's Cathedral, around which booksellers clustered on Paternoster Row.

Religious Atmosphere

Of great significance for the times was religion. Under Elizabeth, a state church had developed; it was Protestant in nature and was called Anglican (or today, Episcopalian) but it had arisen from Henry VIII's break with the Pope and from a compromise with the Roman Catholics who had gained power under Mary Tudor.

The Church of England was headed by the Archbishop of Canter bury, who was to be an increasingly important figure in the early part of the seventeenth century. There were also many schismatic groups, which generally desired further departures from Roman Catholicism. Calvinists were perhaps the most numerous and important of the Protestant groups. The Puritans, who were Calvinist, desired to "purify" the church of ritual and certain dogmas, but during the 1590's they were lampooned as extremists in dress and conduct.

Political Milieu

During Shakespeare's lifetime there were two monarchs: Elizabeth, 1558-1603, and James I, 1603-1625. Elizabeth was the daughter of Henry VIII and Anne Boleyn, his second wife, who was executed in 1536. After Henry's death, his son by his third wife, Jane Seymore (died in 1537), reigned as Edward VI. He was followed by Mary Tudor, daughter of Henry's first wife, Catherine of Aragon. Mary was a Roman Catholic, who tried to put down religious dissension by persecution of both Protestants and Catholics. Nor did her marriage to Philip II of Spain endear her to the people.

Elizabeth's reign was troubled by many offers of marriage, particularly from Spanish and French nobles — all Roman Catholic — and by the people's concern for an heir to the throne. English suitors generally cancelled one another out by intrigue or aggressiveness. One of the most prominent was the Earl of Essex, Robert Devereux, who fell in and out of favor; he apparently attempted to take over the reins of control, only to be captured, imprisoned and executed in February, 1601. One claimant to the throne was Mary of Scotland, a Roman Catholic and widow of Francis II of France. She was the second cousin of Elizabeth, tracing her claim through her grandmother, who was Henry VIII's sister. Finally, settlement came with Elizabeth's acceptance of Mary's son as heir apparent, though Mary was to be captured, tried and executed for treason in 1587. Mary had abdicated the throne of Scotland in 1567 in favor of her son, James VI. His ascent to the throne of England in 1603 as James I joined the two kingdoms for the first time, although Scotland during the seventeenth century often acted independently of England.

Contemporary Events

Political and religious problems were intermingled in the celebrated Gunpowder Plot. Angry over fines that were levied upon those not attending Church of England services — primarily Roman Catholics — and offended by difficulties over papal envoys, a group of Catholics plotted to blow up Parliament, and James with it, at its first session on November 5, 1605. A cache of gunpowder was stored in the cellar, guarded by various conspirators, among them Guy Fawkes. The plot was discovered before it could be carried out and Fawkes, on duty at the time, was apprehended. The execution of the plotters and the triumph of the anti-Papists led in succeeding years to celebrations in the streets and the hanging of Fawkes in effigy.

Among the most noteworthy public events during these times were the wars with the Spanish, which included the defeat of the Spanish Armada in 1588, the battle in the Lowlands in 1590-1594, the expedition to Cadiz under Essex in 1596 and the expedition to the Azores (the Islands Expedition), also under Essex, in 1597. With trading companies especially set up for colonization and exploitation, travel excited the imagination of the people: here was a new way of life, here were new customs brought back by the sailors and merchants, here was a new dream world to explore.

In all, the years from around 1590 to 1601 were trying ones for English people, relieved only by the news from abroad, the new affluence and the hope for the future under James. Writers of the period frequently reflect, however, the disillusionment and sadness of those difficult times.

The Elizabethan Theater

Appearance

The Elizabethan playhouse developed from the medieval inn with its rooms grouped around a courtyard into which a stage was built. This pattern was used in The Theatre, built by James Burbage in 1576: a square frame building (later round or octagonal) with a square yard, three tiers of galleries, each jutting out over the one below, and a stage extending into the middle of the yard, where people stood or sat on improvised seats. There was no cover over the yard or stage and lighting was therefore natural. Thus performances were what we might consider late matinees or early evening performances; in summer, daylight continues in London until around ten o'clock.

Other theaters were constructed during the ensuing years: The Curtain in 1577, The Rose in 1587 (on Bankside), The Swan in 1595 (also Bankside) and Shakespeare's playhouse, The Globe, in 1599 (not far from The Rose). There is still some question about the exact dimensions of this house, but it seems to have been octagonal, each side measuring about 36 feet, with an over-all diameter of 84 feet. It was about 33 feet to the eaves, and the yard was 56 feet in diameter. Three sides were used for backstage and to serve the needs of the players. There was no curtain or proscenium, hence the spectators became part of the action. Obviously, the actors' asides and soliloquies were effective under these conditions.

There was no real scenery and there were only a few major props; thus the lines of the play had to reveal locations and movement, changes in time or place, etc. In this way, too, it was easier to establish a nonrealistic setting, for all settings were created in words. On either side of the stage were doors, within the flooring were trapdoors (for entrances of ghosts, etc.), and behind the main stage was the inner stage or recess. Here, indoor scenes (such as a court or a bedchamber) were played, and some props could be used because the inner stage was usually concealed by a curtain when not in use. It might also have served to hide someone behind the ever-present arras, like Polonius in *Hamlet*. The "chamber" was on the second level, with windows and a balcony. On the third level was another chamber, primarily for musicians.

Actors

An acting company such as the Lord Chamberlain's Men was a fellowship of ten to fifteen sharers with some ten to twelve extras, three or four boys (often to play women's roles) who might become full sharers, and stagehands. There were rival companies, each with its leading dramatist and leading tragic actor and clown. The Lord Admiral's Men, organized in 1594, boasted Ben Jonson and the tragedian Edward Alleyn. Some of the rivalry of this War of the Theaters is reflected in the speeches of Hamlet, who also comments on the ascendancy and unwarranted popularity of the children's companies (like the Children of Blackfriars) in the late 1590's.

The company dramatist, of course, had to think in terms of the members of his company as he wrote his play. He had to make use of the physical features and peculiar talents of the actors, making sure, besides, that there was a role for each member. The fact that women's parts were taken by boys imposed obvious limitations on the range of action. Accordingly, we often find women characters impersonating men; for example, Robert Goffe played Portia in *The Merchant of Venice*, and Portia impersonates a male lawyer in the important trial scene. Goffe also played Juliet, and Anne in *Richard III*, and Oberon in *Midsummer Night's Dream*. The influence of an actor on the playwright can be seen, on the one hand, by noting the "humor" characters portrayed so competently by Thomas Pope, who was a choleric Mercutio in *Romeo*, a melancholic Jaques in *As You Like It*, and a sanguinary Falstaff in *Henry IV*, Part I; and by comparing, on the other hand, the clown Bottom in *Midsummer Night's Dream*, played in a frolicsome manner by William Kempe, with the clown Feste in *Twelfth Night*, sung and danced by Robert Armin. Obviously, too, if a certain kind of character was not available within the company, then that kind of character could not be written into the play. The approach was decidedly different from ours today, where the play almost always comes first and the casting of roles second. The plays were performed in a repertory system, with a different play each afternoon. The average life of a play was about ten performances.

History of the Drama

English drama goes back to native forms developed from playlets presented at Church holidays. Mystery plays dealt with biblical stories

10

such as the Nativity or the Passion, and miracle plays usually depicted the lives of saints. The merchant and craft guilds that came to own and produce the cycles of plays were the forerunners of the theatrical companies of Shakespeare's time. The kind of production these cycles received, either as moving pageants in the streets or as staged shows in a churchyard, influenced the late sixteenth-century production of a secular play: there was an intimacy with the audience and there was a great reliance on words rather than setting and props. Similar involvement with the stage action is experienced by audiences of the arena theater of today.

The morality play, the next form to develop, was an allegory of the spiritual conflict between good and evil in the soul of man. The *dramatis personae* were abstract virtues and vices, with at least one man representing Mankind (or Everyman, as the most popular of these plays was titled). Some modern critics see *Othello* as a kind of morality play in which the soul of Othello is vied for by the aggressively evil Iago (as a kind of Satanic figure) and passively good Desdemona (as a personification of Christian faith in all men). The Tudor interlude — a short, witty, visual play — may have influenced the subplot of the Elizabethan play with its low-life and jesting and visual tricks. In mid-sixteenth century appeared the earliest known English comedies, Nicholas Udall's *Ralph Roister Doister* and *Gammer Gurton's Needle* (of uncertain authorship). Both show the influence of the Roman comic playwright Plautus. Shakespeare's *Comedy of Errors*, performed in the 1590's, was an adaptation of Plautus' *Menaechmi*, both plays featuring twins and an involved story of confused identities. The influence of the Roman tragedian Seneca can be traced from Thomas Norton and Thomas Sackville in *Gorboduc* to *Hamlet*. Senecan tragedy is a tragedy of revenge, characterized by many deaths, much blood-letting, ghosts, feigned madness and the motif of a death for a death.

Shakespeare's Artistry

Plots

Generally, a Shakespearean play has two plots: a main plot and a subplot. The subplot reflects the main plot and is often concerned with inferior characters. Two contrasting examples will suffice: Lear and his daughters furnish the characters for the main plot of filial love and ingratitude, whereas Gloucester and his sons enact the same theme in the subplot; Lear and Gloucester both learn that outward signs of love may be false. In *Midsummer Night's Dream*, the town workmen (Quince, Bottom *et al.*) put on a tragic play in such a hilarious way that it turns the subject of the play — love so strong that the hero will kill himself if his loved one dies first — into farce, but this in the main plot is the "serious" plight of the four mixed-up lovers. In both examples Shakespeare has reinforced his points by subplots dealing with the same subject as the main plot.

11

Sources

The plots of the Elizabethan plays were usually adapted from other sources. "Originality" was not the sought quality; a kind of variation on a theme was. It was felt that one could better evaluate the playwright's worth by seeing what he did with a familiar tale. What he stressed, how he stressed it, how he restructured the familiar elements — these were the important matters. Shakespeare closely followed Sir Thomas North's very popular translation of Plutarch's *Life of Marcus Antonius*, for example, in writing *Antony and Cleopatra*; and he modified Robert Greene's *Pandosto* and combined it with the Pygmalion myth in *The Winter's Tale*, while drawing the character of Autolycus from certain pamphlets written by Greene. The only plays for which sources have not been clearly determined are *Love's Labour's Lost* (probably based on contemporary events) and *The Tempest* (possibly based on some shipwreck account from travellers to the New World).

Verse and Prose

There is a mixture of verse and prose in the plays, partially because plays fully in verse were out of fashion. Greater variety could thus be achieved and character or atmosphere could be more precisely delineated. Elevated passages, philosophically significant ideas, speeches by men of high rank are in verse, but comic and light parts, speeches including dialect or broken English, and scenes that move more rapidly or simply give mundane information are in prose. The poetry is almost always blank verse (iambic pentameter lines without rhyme). Rhyme is used, however (particularly the couplet), to mark the close of scenes or an important action. Rhyme also serves as a cue for the entrance of another actor or some off-stage business, to point to a change of mood or thought, as a forceful opening after a passage of prose, to convey excitement or passion or sentimentality and to distinguish characters.

Shakespeare's plays may be divided into three general categories, though some plays are not readily classified and further subdivisions may be suggested within a category.

The History Play

The history play, or chronicle, may tend to tragedy, like *Richard II*, or to comedy, like *Henry IV*, Part I. It is a chronicle of some royal personage, often altered for dramatic purposes, even to the point of falsification of the facts. Its popularity may have resulted from the rising of nationalism of the English, nurtured by their successes against the Spanish, their developing trade and colonization, and their rising prestige as a world power. The chronicle was considered a political guide, like the popular *Mirror for Magistrates*, a collection of writings showing what happens when an important leader falls through some error in his ways, his thinking or his personality. Thus the history play counseled the right path by negative, if not positive, means. Accordingly, it is difficult to call *Richard II* a tragedy, since Richard was wrong and his wrongness harmed his people. The political philosophy of Shakespeare's day seemed to favor the view that all usurpation was bad and should be corrected, but not by further usurpation. When that original usurpation had been established, through an heir's ascension to the throne, it was to be accepted. Then any rebellion against the "true" king would be a rebellion against God.

Tragedy

Tragedy in simple terms meant that the protagonist died. Certain concepts drawn from Aristotle's *Poetics* require a tragic hero of high standing, who must oppose some conflicting force, either external or internal. The tragic hero should be dominated by a *hamartia* (a so-called tragic flaw, but really an *excess* of some character trait, e.g., pride, or *hubris*), and it is this *hamartia* that leads to his downfall and, because of his status, to the downfall of others. The action presented in the tragedy must be recognizable to the audience as real and potential: through seeing it enacted, the audience has its passion (primarily suffering) raised, and the conclusion of the action thus brings release from that passion (*catharsis*). A more meaningful way of looking at tragedy in the Elizabethan theater, however, is to see it as that which occurs when essential good (like Hamlet) is wasted (through disaster or death) in the process of driving out evil (such as Claudius represents).

Comedy

Comedy in simple terms meant that the play ended happily for the protagonists. Sometimes the comedy depends on exaggerations of man's eccentricities — comedy of humors; sometimes the comedy is romantic and far-fetched. The romantic comedy was usually based on a mix-up in events or confused identity of characters, particularly by disguise. It moved toward tragedy in that an important person might die and the mix-up might never be unraveled; but in the nick of time something happens or someone appears (sometimes illogically or unexpectedly) and saves the day. It reflects the structure of myth by moving from happiness to despair to resurrection. *The Winter's Tale* is a perfect example of this, for the happiness of the first part is banished with Hermione's exile and Perdita's abandonment; tragedy is near when the lost baby, Perdita, cannot be found and Hermione is presumed dead, but Perdita re-appears, as does Hermione, a statue that suddenly comes to life. Lost identities are established and confusions disappear but the mythic-comic nature of the play is seen in the reuniting of the mother, Hermione, a kind of Ceres, with her daughter, Perdita, a kind of Prosperina. Spring returns, summer will bring the harvest, and the winter of the tale is left behind — for a little while.

What is it, then, that makes Shakespeare's art so great? Perhaps we see in it a whole spectrum of humanity, treated impersonally, but with kindness and understanding. We seldom meet in Shakespeare a weeping philosopher: he may criticize, but he criticizes both sides. After he has done so, he gives the impression of saying, Well, that's the way life is; people will always be like that — don't get upset about it. This is probably the key to the Duke's behavior in *Measure for Measure* — a most unbitter comedy despite former labels. Only in *Hamlet* does Shakespeare not seem to fit this statement; it is the one play that Shakespeare, the person, enters.

As we grow older and our range of experience widens, so, too, does Shakespeare's range seem to expand. Perhaps this lies in the ambiguities of his own materials, which allow for numerous individual readings. We meet our own experiences — and they are ours alone, we think — expressed in phrases that we thought our own or of our own discovery. What makes Shakespeare's art so great, then, is his ability to say so much to so many people in such memorable language: he is himself "the show and gaze o' the time."

MACBETH
Plot Summary

ACT I

Macbeth has subdued first a rebellion and then an invasion of Scotland by Norwegian troops assisted by a traitor, the Thane of Cawdor. Accompanied by his fellow commander Banquo, he meets three witches on his way back from battle. They greet him as the Thane of Glamis, as the Thane of Cawdor, and as the future king. When he starts back affrighted, Banquo asks the witches what the future holds in store for him. They inform him that he will found a line of kings although he himself will not be king. Macbeth challenges them, pointing out that he does not have the title of Thane of Cawdor, but when two noblemen arrive with the message that the king has divested the traitor of this title to confer it upon him, Macbeth is shaken by the verification of the witches' words and by the horrible thought of murder which comes to him.

Macbeth is graciously received by King Duncan, who as a mark of his favor announces that he will visit Macbeth in his castle. At the castle, Lady Macbeth, informed of the witches' prophecy by a letter from her husband, expresses fear that Macbeth will not have the ruthlessness to do what is necessary to become king. When Macbeth, after his arrival expresses reluctance to commit murder, she urges him on and prevails.

ACT II

Macbeth, summoning up all his will power, goes to kill the sleeping Duncan. Lady Macbeth waits tensely for his return. When he comes back, it is with blood on his hands and horror in his soul. She urges him to wash the blood off and goes to lay the bloody daggers by the side of the sleeping grooms in order that the suspicion of the murder fall on them.

Macduff, a nobleman appointed to wake Duncan, enters his bed-chamber and rouses the occupants of the castle with his cries. Macbeth rushes to the chamber and kills the grooms, pretending to be carried away by anger. Malcolm and Donalbain, the king's sons, suspicious and fearful, decide to run away, Malcolm to England and Donalbain to Ireland. By doing so, they themselves incur suspicion. Macbeth is chosen king by the council of noblemen and proceeds to the coronation.

ACT III

Macbeth, now king, has a banquet to which he invites Banquo, whom he fears. Macbeth is also tormented by his recollection of the prophecy that Banquo will be the father of kings, a prophecy which implies that he himself will not found a dynasty. He plans to have Banquo and his young son Fleance murdered on their way to the banquet, but Fleance runs away as the assassins fall upon his father. At the banquet Macbeth is dismayed when, on his expressing his regret at the absence of Banquo, the ghost of Banquo, seen only by himself, appears. He speaks wildly to it, amazing everyone. Lady Macbeth attempts to reassure the company, saying that Macbeth has been subject to such seizures since his youth. Finally, however, the company has to be asked to leave. The nobility now suspects Macbeth, and we are told that Macduff has gone to join Malcolm in England.

ACT IV

Macbeth, resolved to know what the future has in store for him, goes to see the witches again. They summon apparitions who tell him that he should beware of Macduff, that no man born of woman will harm him, and that he will not be vanquished until Birnam Wood comes to Dunsinane Hill. When he asks them, however, whether Banquo's issue will ever reign in Scotland, they show him a procession of kings, which the ghost of Banquo points to as his. Infuriated by the sight, Macbeth, on being told immediately thereafter that Macduff has fled to England, has Lady Macduff and her young son killed.

In England, Macduff has sought out Malcolm to tell him how Macbeth is bringing new sorrows to his country every day and to urge him to levy an army against the tyrant. Malcolm, to make sure that Macduff is not an agent of Macbeth, accuses himself of sins which make him unfit to rule. When Macduff turns away in despair, Malcolm informs him that he spoke only to test him and that he is preparing to lead an expedition against Macbeth. At this moment the nobleman Ross comes to tell Macduff of the murder of his wife and children. At first, Macduff is overcome by grief, but he resolves to kill Macbeth when he meets him on the field of battle.

ACT V

Lady Macbeth, like Macbeth, has been suffering inner torments, and we see her walking in her sleep, reenacting the murder of Duncan and seeking in vain to wash the blood off her hands. As Macbeth, frantic, is preparing to be besieged in his castle at Dunsinane, he is told that his wife has committed suicide, but life is now a meaningless thing for him, and he spends no time lamenting.

In the meantime, Malcolm has ordered that each of his men cut off a bough from Birnam Wood and bear it before him as they advance so that it will be difficult for enemy scouts to determine the size of the army. A soldier who has been standing guard on top of the hill runs to Macbeth to tell him that he saw Birnam Wood moving. Macbeth, who has been relying on the supposed assurance of the witches, orders his men in the frenzy of his despair to leave the castle and attack: at least they will die in battle.

Attacking with the desperate courage of a trapped animal, Macbeth now relies on the assurance that no man born of woman can hurt him. Although his men readily surrender, he continues to fight, determined to continue killing rather than to commit suicide. The sight of Macduff, however, takes him aback, for his soul is burdened by the slaying of Lady Macduff and her children. Macbeth fights, nevertheless, when Macduff attacks him, telling Macduff that his efforts are in vain, for he is fighting against one who cannot be hurt by a man born of woman. When Macduff replies that he was "from his mother's womb/Untimely ripped," Macbeth is momentarily cowed, but he will not yield and dies fighting.

Sources

The major and perhaps only source of *Macbeth* is Raphael Holinshed's *Chronicles of England, Scotlande and Irelande* (1577), which was also a major source for Shakespeare's English history plays and a source for portions of *King Lear* and *Cymbeline*. Scholars have argued for other works as additional sources for *Macbeth,* but it is often hard to say whether or not a supposed parallel is merely a coincidence and a supposed verbal echo is merely a use of a commonplace of the time. At all events, it is clear that Shakespeare's chief indebtedness is to Holinshed's history.

Here Shakespeare found most of the detail for his tragedy. The most significant changes that he made were as follows: many of the facts in the murder of Shakespeare's Duncan come not from Holinshed's account of that murder but from his account of the murder of another King, Duff, by the nobleman Donwald and his wife; Macbeth's character is blackened; Banquo, on the other hand, is cleared of guilt. What Shakespeare evidently sought to do was to make Macbeth's crime as heinous as possible. Therefore, instead of using the facts of the killing of Duncan, an assassination that was done in the open, he uses those of the murder done by Donwald, who was host of Duff, drugged his grooms, and put on a display of innocence and indignation. Donwald had the aid, however, of four servants, and this Shakespeare omitted in order to focus on Macbeth and fasten full responsibility on him. Furthermore, in Holinshed Macbeth had reason to feel aggrieved against Duncan, and Duncan was not an old, saintly king but a young, feeble one.

What Shakespeare therefore did was, with the audacity of genius, to make it as difficult as possible for himself to gain the audience's sympathy for Macbeth. Yet he succeeded magnificently in doing so by causing the audience to appreciate the intensity of his temptation, to perceive the power of evil, and above all to share his terrors. Banquo, who was supposed to be the ancestor of Shakespeare's own King James, Shakespeare makes a foil for Macbeth. In Holinshed he was one of Macbeth's accomplices in the assassination of Duncan, but Shakespeare makes him resist evil in contrast with Macbeth, who succumbs to it.

Scottish Historical Background

During the tenth century the united kingdoms of Scotland, known as Alban, comprised the land north of the Firths of Forth and Clyde. Malcolm II (1005-34) and his grandson Duncan I (1034-40) added the lands south to Solway Firth and the Tweed River. Attempted invasion by the Norsemen, who had acquired footholds in the various islands surrounding Scotland, was repulsed during Duncan's reign. Macbeth, the steward (*mormaor*) of Ross and Moray, ended much of the internal strife in 1040 when he assassinated the king and assumed the throne. In 1057 he was defeated by Duncan's son, who ascended the throne as Malcolm III, ruling until his death in 1093. His reign was significant for its transformation of Celtic culture into English culture and the influence of Roman Catholicism through Malcolm's English wife Margaret.

The world of *Macbeth* is a world of an early feudalism which has barely managed to establish a precarious social order. This world in the rocky highlands of Scotland is hard and primitive, abounding in violence. But in this world Macbeth is a heroic figure (at first), a valiant warrior loyally serving his king. He disdains the fortune of battle that seemed to smile upon the rebel and wins despite it by his heroic deeds. Such valor is rewarded by the king by title and land, and the crown itself was not at this time hereditary. A council of nobles would elect a new king from among the members of the royal family after the death of the previous king. However, a successor was frequently declared in the lifetime of the reigning king, and in such an event the title of Prince of Cumberland was given to him. The formal conferral of the title upon Malcolm would have meant that the nobility had recognized him as heir-apparent.

From Holinshed Shakespeare got a picture of a primitive feudalism still attempting to impose social order, of violent acts, black treachery, and oppressive remorse. This cultural setting contributes to the distinctive atmosphere of *Macbeth,* with its gloomy castles able to "laugh a siege to scorn," its boding ravens, heavily barred gates, alarum bells that call to arms, barren heaths, and savage hand-to-hand conflicts.

However, while removing the tragedies from the here and now, Shakespeare generally made use of references to the things of his day. These were once decried as anachronisms that were the result of either his ignorance or his carelessness, but they are now seen as artistic means by which Shakespeare made the events of the past have relevance to the present and made the events of the present have a universal significance. In this, *Macbeth* is like Shakespeare's other tragedies.

Topicality

The Scottish setting of *Macbeth* gave it an immediate topical appeal. The date of its first performance has generally been placed by scholars in 1606. In 1603 James VI of Scotland ascended to the throne and became James I of England. There had been a great deal of anxiety concerning who was to be the successor to Elizabeth, and when James became king without bloodshed there was general relief. The prophecy that Banquo's descendants would not only hold the kingdom of Scotland but would join it with that of England in a union that would be ruled by his line into the indefinite future would therefore have accorded with the atmosphere of the time.

The presence of the witches in *Macbeth,* although they are derived from Holinshed, also has a special topical significance, for James was convinced that he was the victim of witchcraft. His mortal enemy, his cousin the younger Bothwell, was convicted of seeking to cause his death through witchcraft. James also attributed to witchcraft the great storms that repeatedly drove back the ship bringing his bride from Denmark. He himself interrogated old women charged with being witches and elicited from them confessions to having performed such impossibilities as going to sea in sieves such as the witches speak of in *Macbeth*.

Most important of all the topical references, however, is that of the Porter to the equivocator who committed treason in God's name but could not equivocate his way to heaven. This alludes to Father Garnet, who in the Gunpowder Plot trial was charged with having made use of the Jesuit doctrine of equivocation that permitted one to swear under duress something to which he made internal mental reservations. The Gunpowder Plot, which sought to destroy at one blow king and parliament, made a terrific impact on the popular imagination, so much so that its discovery is still celebrated in England as Guy Fawkes Day. The Scottish Privy Council proclaimed that it was diabolically inspired. James compared it in its heinousness to the sensational murder of his father, between which and the murder of Duff, used by Shakespeare in his representation of the murder of Duncan, contemporary historians drew parallels. In short, the violence permeating *Macbeth* is not merely the violence of primitive Scotland; it is also the violence of Renaissance Scotland and Renaissance England, and it would have been perceived as such. This perception would have brought home to Shakespeare's audience that the struggle between good and evil is an everlasting one.

By using our historical imaginations, we can appreciate how the charged atmosphere of Shakespeare's time affected the audience's response to *Macbeth*. Such an appreciation can heighten its meaningfulness for us. The perception of how Shakespeare universalized the contemporary may indeed suggest parallels with our own day, such as a comparison between Macbeth and a dictator like Stalin, who like Macbeth betrayed his own early principles, became paranoic and suspicious of everyone as a threat to his power, indulged in blood purges, kept an army of spies and secret agents, and killed members of the families of those who had defected or been exiled. The knowledge of the Elizabethan Shakespeare makes him come alive in the twentieth century.

The Witches

Witches were not a Hallowe'en joke in Shakespeare's day. They and other manifestations of the supernatural were widely believed in, probably by almost everyone, educated as well as uneducated. The beginnings of modern rationalism were at work, for Reginald Scot wrote a book attacking belief in witches, but the shocked response of James I, who ordered the book burned and wrote one of his own in reply, was doubtless typical.

Shakespeare gave his "weird sisters" the customary features of witches of his day. They have animals—a cat, a toad—who are really "familiars," evil spirits who have taken this bodily form. They arrange to meet in a thunderstorm, as if they can affect the weather, as they were supposed to be able to do. There is frequent reference to the owl, a customary "familiar" of witches. Macbeth has bad dreams, and these were notoriously caused by witches, as were such hallucinations as the "air-drawn dagger." Indeed the very word "nightmare," often also called in Shakespeare's time "night hag" or "the riding of the witch," refers to a witch riding wildly through the night on horseback, visiting bad dreams on her victims.

What, however, are the limits of the powers of the witches and from where do they derive these powers? On these points there was confusion in popular and learned belief. Witches could be regarded as old women who were given supernatural powers by the devil, to whom they had sold their souls, or as demons who had assumed the bodies of old women for their evil purposes. They were also identified with the classical furies, who were goddesses of punishment, and with fairies and elves, creatures of folklore who were more sinister than we think of them today. Some writers called witches "weirds" (derived from an old English word meaning "fate"), and Holinshed, in giving one explanation of the three women who met Macbeth (another is that they are "nymphs or fairies, endued with knowledge of prophecy") used "weird sisters" to refer to "the goddesses of destiny," the Parcae of classical mythology or the Norns of Scandinavian mythology.

Shakespeare's witches are a compound of native folklore and classical mythology. They are called the weird sisters throughout the play except by the sailor's wife and in the stage-directions, where they are referred to as witches. They serve demons, for they are summoned by their "familiars" and conjure up apparitions whom they call masters. Their use of cauldrons for divination is borrowed from the practice of classical furies, not from that of native witches. They are associated with Hecate, the Greek goddess of sorcery and the other world, who is referred to in portions of the play other than the non-Shakespearean interpolations in which she appears.

Although the witches can foretell the future, the general tenor of the play suggests that Macbeth bears responsibility for his own actions, that they can strongly tempt and influence him but are not in control of his destiny. There is, to be sure, an air of fatalism in the predestined role of Macduff, but fundamentally Macbeth brings his own doom upon himself in being driven by the torments of his own sense of guilt into a fearful insecurity that causes him to commit further guilty crimes. His crucial decision to kill Lady Macduff and her children is his own, although the witches could foresee that, once having attempted to escape the consequences of his guilt through further crime, he would land in that final trap.

The sharpest expression of the free will of the two central characters is Lady Macbeth's invocation of evil spirits. She deliberately chooses evil as her good. Elizabethans would have regarded her as literally possessed by the spirits she has summoned. Similarly, Macbeth chooses to murder

Duncan and does not blame the witches for having made this choice. He only blames them later for having deceived him with false promises. He is tempted by the forces of evil and driven to despair by them when he succumbs, losing his soul, but his soul is his own to keep or lose.

We no longer believe in witches, but we can give dramatic credence to them, for if we do not believe in "the riding of the witch," we still have nightmares. Moreover, in giving dramatic credence to them, we can recognize them and the devil they serve as symbolic of the evil to which men succumb. Paraphrasing an ancient question, we may say, "What does it profit a man to gain the kingdom of Scotland and lose his own personal integrity?" As long as men do evil to others and betray their own principles, as long as there is war and injustice, the witches' hell-brew still bubbles.

A Note on the Text

The only authoritative text of *Macbeth* is that of the First Folio (1623). It is apparently an acting version, abridged and changed from its original form and augmented by scenes or songs written by Thomas Middleton. Abridgment is suggested by the lack of a substantial subplot and by the fact that this is the shortest of Shakespeare's tragedies. Alterations are evidenced by prosodic and punctuational problems. However, the substantive text does not seem to be corrupt. Middleton's additions, taken from his play *The Witch* (ca. 1612), are the scenes involving Hecate and the witches' songs: Act III, Sc. 5; Act IV, Sc. 1, 38-43, 125-132.

Stage History

The first reference to *Macbeth* is a note by the astrologer Dr. Simon Forman that he saw it enacted at the Globe on April 20, 1611. Richard Burbage (1567?-1619), "the English Roscius," created the title role. The Restoration saw a revision of the tragedy into a kind of opera with flying witches and dancing, by Sir William Davenant, who had received a royal warrant for various Shakespearean plays at the end of 1660. John Downes tells us in *Roscius Anglicanus* (1708) that the Duke's Theatre (Dorset Garden) production in 1673 "recompensed double the expense" of all the new finery and scenery and machines. At times the text was "reformed" to remove Shakespeare's indecorousness and obscurity: for example, the "cream-fac'd loon" becomes a "Friend," and a "goose look" becomes a "change of countenance." The leading actor of the Duke's Company, Thomas Betterton (1635?-1710), played Macbeth, and first his wife, Mrs. Saunderson (?-1711), and then Elizabeth Barry (1658-1713) undertook Lady Macbeth. This version held the stage until 1744 with such men as Robert Wilks (1665?-1732) in the lead.

David Garrick revised the play to restore much of its tragic qualities in the Drury Lane presentation of 1743 except that he added a rather sentimental dying speech for Macbeth in which he lamented his fate. Hannah Pritchard (1711-1768) was the most renowned interpreter of Lady Macbeth during this time; she acted in Garrick's company. In 1773 Charles

Macklin (1697?-1797) gave his audience actors in kilts against a setting placed in the Highlands. John Philip Kemble (1757-1823), a fine Macbeth, returned to the singing and dancing witches of Davenant's version while retaining Garrick's speech for the dying hero. He was joined by his sister, the fabled Sarah Siddons (1775-1831), as Lady Macbeth in this Drury Lane production of 1794. Later his witches became more truly evil spirits writhing in blackness.

The nineteenth century saw such significant performances of the play as William Charles Macready's (1793-1873) in a fuller restoring of Shakespeare's text; Samuel Phelps' (1804-1878) in 1847; Henry Irving's (1838-1905) in 1888; and Johnston Forbes-Robertson's (1853-1937) in 1898. The lavish production of Herbert Beerbohm Tree (1853-1917) in 1911 was not yet really twentieth-century in style. The opera by Verdi with a libretto fairly close to Shakespeare has been revived most successfully in recent years. The play has been popular as a vehicle for major actors and, of course, with all the Festival groups. Part of its popularity with the general public, however, stems from its being standard school reading. Notable renditions have been those of Lyn Harding and Florence Reed in 1928; of Maurice Evans and Judith Anderson in 1941; and of Michael Redgrave and Flora Robson in 1948. Orson Welles put the play on film in 1948; and television has frequently offered an abbreviated version with Evans and Anderson.

Summaries and Commentaries
By Act and Scene

ACT I • SCENE 1

Summary

Amid thunder and lightning three witches make a rendezvous for the purpose of encountering Macbeth after a battle now raging has been concluded. The place of this scene is not specified: we may imagine any desolate spot, as "wither'd" and "wild" as the witches' attire. They agree to meet again on the heath, an open region devoid of vegetation that is apparently a different place from this one.

Commentary

The keynote of the play is struck with the appearance of the three witches. "Hurlyburly" signifies tumult and confusion, that of battle as well as the murder of Duncan, a violation of natural law bringing unnatural confusion and disorder. This slighting term also suggests the contemptuous regard the witches have for the affairs of men. So does "When the battle's lost and won" (4). Every battle is lost by one side and won by the other, but the witches are indifferent as to which it is that does the losing and the winning. The words also have another meaning: Macbeth will win the battle, but he will lose at this time of triumph another, more important battle—that for his soul.

"Fair is foul, and foul is fair" (11) indicates that everything is unnaturally reversed in the world of evil and that everything is ambiguous and uncertain. Nothing is what it seems to be. The unnatural reversal is seen in the fact that the witches are summoned by Graymalkin (a cat), Paddock (a toad) and an unnamed third creature, animals inhabited by evil spirits. These "pets" call them; the pets, as would be normal, are not called by their mistresses. "Fog and filthy air" (12) depicts an atmosphere of confusion in which deceitful evil operates. Wherever the witches meet, however, will be the barrenness of chaos, for evil is sterile and opposed to the plenteousness of nature.

ACT I • SCENE 2

Summary
King Duncan is told by a captain who has just come from the battle how it proceeded. For a time the issue seemed doubtful. Then the rebel Macdonwald seemed to be winning, but Macbeth made his way to him in battle and slew him. Next, the Norwegian invader made a fresh assault. At this point the strength of the captain, weakened by his wounds, gives out, and he is helped away. The Thane of Ross comes with the latest news of the battle. Again, it seemed as if the Norwegian forces, outnumbering the Scottish, were on the verge of winning, but Macbeth finally carried the day. Duncan announces that the Thane of Cawdor, a traitor who secretly assisted Norway, will be executed and sends Ross to tell Macbeth that the title of the Thane of Cawdor is now his.

Commentary
LINES 1-45
The first scene, with its thunder and lightning and the startling appearance of the witches, is designed to attract the audience's attention. Having done so, Shakespeare proceeds to his task of exposition.

The captain's account of the battle is full of images of blood, one of the pervading images in the poetry as well as literally on the stage. The captain himself is a "bloody man" (1), whose "gashes" (43) cause him almost to faint at the end of his speech. Macbeth's sword "smok'd" with "bloody execution" (18); that is, it steamed with the hot blood which it had caused to gush. To reach Macdonwald, Macbeth sliced his way through the men in the front lines (19) as if he were a butcher carving meat. He "unseam'd" Macdonwald "from the nave to th' chops" (22) and Macbeth and Banquo, fighting savagely against the Norwegians, seemed to intend to bathe in the hot blood spouting forth (40). In this world of violence Macbeth is a heroic figure.

If Fortune appeared to be the "whore" (15) of the rebel Macdonwald—Fortune (or, as we sometimes say now, Lady Luck) was personified in Shakespeare's time as a woman whose fickleness often caused her to be called a harlot—Macbeth was "Bellona's bridegroom" (55), married in his martial splendor to the goddess of war. However, he, who here disdains fortune, becomes preoccupied with what is in store for him in the future when evil makes use of his ambition. He, who "fix'd" the rebel Macdonwald's "head upon our battlements" (23), will at the end have his own head held up for display.

LINES 46-69
The last words of the scene, referring to the transfer of Cawdor's title to Macbeth, recall the witches' "When the battle's lost and won." The battle, which had seemed so uncertain, had finally been won by Macbeth. With it he has won a new title—but it was the title of a traitor, and he himself will shortly be false to the king. He defeats two external threats to the kingdom of Scotland but will succumb to the third threat, that within himself.

ACT I • SCENE 3

Summary
The three witches appear on the heath in the midst of thunder. Waiting for Macbeth, they tell each other of their misdeeds. The first witch, out of vengeance against a sailor's wife, who would not give her the chestnuts she asked for, had given the sailor contrary winds so that he could not make port but sailed for eighty-one weeks without sleep. Macbeth and Banquo enter. Banquo, amazed at the uncanny appearance of the witches, addresses them. They hail Macbeth as the Thane of Glamis and Cawdor who will be king and hail Banquo as one who is lesser than Macbeth and yet greater, less fortunate and yet more fortunate. When Macbeth asks the witches how can he be Thane of Cawdor, since the holder of that title still lives, and it is therefore as unbelievable that he is Cawdor as it is that he will be king, the witches vanish. At this moment Ross enters to announce the new title that Duncan has given Macbeth. Macbeth is thunderstruck, and horrible imaginings come to his mind. Banquo reacts to this news with "What! can the Devil speak true?" (107), but answers himself soon afterwards, with words that Macbeth would have done well to heed, "Oftentimes, to win us to our harm, The instruments of Darkness tell us truths" (123-24). He disregards Banquo's words and accepts the prophecy as an invitation to evil, such as the "horrid image" of himself murdering Duncan, which causes his hair to stand on end and his heart to pound unnaturally. The image is so overwhelming that his powers of action are made incapable of functioning in his contemplation of what seems to be the future. Recalled to himself, Macbeth excuses his abstractedness by saying that he was trying to recall something which had slipped from his mind.

Commentary
LINES 1-37
Modern audiences often find it difficult to respond to the witches and are inclined to laugh at them in amusement. They are intended indeed to be grotesque but also to be foully redolent of evil, and yet if their spite is petty,

they have the power to cause the ship of a sailor whose wife offended them to be tempest-tossed for "weary sev'n-nights nine times nine" (22). The cursed sailor is unable to sleep during this time, as Macbeth will later be unable to sleep. There is, however, a suggestion that their powers are limited: the sailor's ship "cannot be lost" (24). Since life was often compared to a voyage, the powers of evil can cause life's voyage to have a rough ocean, but their malevolence cannot cause a good man to lose his soul. Having sold themselves to the devil, they play a role in God's scheme of things, testing men by tempting them to evil, but they cannot control the future, which is ruled by divine providence.

LINES 38-88

Macbeth's words as he and Banquo enter—"So foul and fair a day I have not seen" (38)—have several possible meanings. The sentence is purposefully ambiguous. Macbeth may simply be commenting on the changeableness of the weather, which has suddenly become foggy in the presence of the as yet unseen witches; or he may be saying that he has never seen a battle whose outcome was so uncertain, first appearing to be unhappy or foul and then appearing to be happy or fair; or he may be saying that the fair victory and the foul weather are in sharp contrast. Each of these meanings relates to the uncertainty of things. There is, moreover, a further meaning of which he is unaware: his words echo the witches' "Fair is foul, and foul is fair," suggesting that the witches, unknown to Macbeth, have already established a connection between them. Ironically, he does not know how foul a day this will prove to be for him.

The theme of the difficulty of distinguishing between what is appearance and what is reality is played upon throughout this drama. This reflects the evil which, though hidden, is always lurking in wait for us. It is specifically raised in Banquo's questioning of the witches. Questions suggest the confusion, uncertainty, and mystery which pervades the play.

The difference between Macbeth and Banquo is noteworthy. When the witches prophesy that Macbeth shall be king, he starts as if in fear. The suggestion is that they give utterance to his own secret thought. When they vanish instead of answering him, he exclaims (82) "Would they had stay'd!" Banquo, however, is surprised by Macbeth's response to what seems "so fair" (52), not knowing that fair words have provoked foul thoughts. The witches knew that Macbeth was ready to be tempted, and his guilty start and absorption in their words testify to that readiness. Banquo, however, true to his words, is not carried away by the witches' prophecy to him, secure as he is in the staunchness of his soul.

LINES 89-157

When Macbeth hears himself hailed by Ross as the Thane of Cawdor, he replies with an image of himself dressed in the garments of another man (108-9), a recurrent image, as in lines 145-147 of this scene. It is a picture of Macbeth as a usurper: the kingship which he will takes does not belong to him.

The bodily effect of the image which the prophecy of his kingship raises in him rests upon a tenet of contemporary logic; that is, correspondence. The Elizabethans believed the human body to be a microcosm, a little world analogous to the universe, and analogous also to the "body politic," human society, which is organized on the same principle of natural order as the body and the universe. Violation of the natural order of society by the killing of a king was thought to result in disorder in the other two spheres, and throughout the play it is suggested, as here, that Macbeth's own body is in unnatural rebellion against him. The very idea of murder "shakes" his "single state of man" (140), his mind and body, which should be, like the political state, an integrated unity.

In the battle, we have been told, Macbeth was "nothing afeard" of what he himself made. The actual corpses which he created seemed unreal in their dreadfulness. He was undismayed by these, too intent on inflicting death to be afraid of it. The corpse which he sees only in his imagination, however, seems overpoweringly real and causes him to tremble violently. But then, the killings on the battle-field were performed in accordance with his duty as a soldier fighting for his king; the murder he sees in his imagination is a murder of the king in violation of his duty. Proceeding, Macbeth finds only his imagination real (142), another aspect of the theme of the difference between appearance and reality. And it is only through his powerful imagination that his conscience works. At various times in the play, as here, he seems to be living in a hideous dream. The reason he offers for his distractedness is a lie, but in one sense what he says may be true: his mind has been seeking to subdue previously repressed thoughts which the witches' prophecy had caused to re-emerge into his consciousness.

ACT I • SCENE 4

Summary

In the palace at Forres, Duncan is informed of the execution of the former Thane of Cawdor. He comments that one cannot tell the disposition of a man's mind from his face and that he had absolute trust in Cawdor. As he is in the middle of his sentence, Macbeth enters and is greeted with effusive thanks by Duncan. Duncan announces that he will make Malcolm heir to the throne. Macbeth in an aside states that this announcement is a bar to his ambition and calls upon darkness to cover what he wishes to be done. He goes on to call upon his eyes to wink upon what his hand does so that when they open again that which they fear to see will have been done. The King as a mark of his favor proposes to visit Macbeth's castle at Inverness, and Macbeth rides on ahead to prepare a hospitable reception for him.

Commentary

LINES 1-47

The scene shows how ironically Duncan is deceived in Macbeth, as he had been in the previous Thane of Cawdor. History repeats itself because evil, although masked, is an abiding reality in human nature. Duncan is a gracious old king, overflowing with kindliness. His use of imagery of planting and tilling (28-29) is indicative of his bounteousness and suggests, moreover, the naturalness of the relationship between the king and his subjects. "I have begun to plant thee" refers to his recent conferral on Macbeth of the title of Thane of Cawdor. The familiar "thou" instead of the more formal "you" indicates Duncan's affection towards his relative, who is the savior of his kingdom. If Macbeth had not destroyed himself by murdering Duncan to gain the kingship, he would have continued to grow in honor, the true honor which comes from the public recognition of good deeds, for Duncan would have labored to make him "full of growing."

Before Duncan's announcement that Malcolm will be declared Prince of Cumberland, Macbeth might well have had reason to hope that he, rather than the young and inexperienced Malcolm, would have been chosen by the electors. In his joy over Macbeth's victories, therefore, Duncan is unwittingly bringing his own death upon himself—this, despite the fact that Macbeth would undoubtedly have gained new honor in the general distribution of titles. For Macbeth now feels that murder is the only way in which he can achieve the kingship.

LINES 48-57

In his aside Macbeth calls upon the stars to hide their light. What he is contemplating doing should be done only in the darkness, which throughout the play is symbolic of evil. His "black" desires (51), too evil to be seen, should be hidden in darkness. Darkness as setting and as imagery is suggestive of evil throughout the tragedy.

Macbeth's image of the eyes' winking upon the work of the hand is expressive both of his intense aversion to the deed and of his intense desire to get what the deed will accomplish. At the same time his "let that be" (52) marks the point at which his fascinated contemplation of the thought of murdering Duncan becomes a resolution, although he will waver from it. The opposition between eye and hand is indicative of the civil war within him.

Ironically unaware of Macbeth's dark thoughts, Duncan, listening to Banquo's praise of Macbeth, says that such praise is a "banquet" (56) to him. Banquets are symbolic at other points in the play of communion and concord—false rather than real—among their participants.

ACT I • SCENE 5

Summary

Lady Macbeth at the castle in Inverness is reading a letter from her husband that tells of his encounter with the witches. She comments that he is ambitious but has too many scruples. At this moment a messenger arrives to inform her that Duncan will be there that very night. She calls upon evil spirits to render her devoid of compunction. Her soliloquy indicates that, although she is guided by the philosophy that there is no such thing as crime, only weakness, she is not so unnatural as to be without human feeling. Her husband arriving on the scene, she hails him by his present and future greatness and, observing his agitated countenance, tells him to hide the thoughts which are disturbing him.

Commentary
LINES 1-30

We are to take Macbeth's letter as written during a stop on his way from the heath to Duncan's palace. His "my dearest partner in greatness" (11-12) indicates his elation at the prophecy as well as his love for his wife, but he does not say that he proposes to do anything to achieve that prophecy.

Lady Macbeth comments shrewdly on her husband's character although in her own excitement she exaggerates what appear to her to be his weaknesses and minimizes what appear to her to be his strengths. She says that he is "not without ambition" (19), but we have seen that he is burning with ambition. She says that he is without the ruthlessness which should accompany ambition, but we have seen him contemplating murder and resolving upon it. Nevertheless he does have scruples which stand in the way of his committing murder. The series of antitheses which she uses to describe him are appropriate in their presentation of the spiritual wrestlings that go on within him before he is vanquished by evil.

Lady Macbeth's values are an inversion of ordinary human values. The conventional virtues are reasons for reproach. She fears Macbeth's nature, not because it is cruel, but on the contrary because it is "too full o' th' milk of human kindness" (17). "Human kindness" means both "those qualities peculiar to mankind" and "compassion," for compassion is absorbed by babies with their mothers' milk so that it becomes a part of their very being. Macbeth has too much of ordinary human nature in him to "catch the nearest way" (18), even though it means passing over human bodies. He was able to hew his way through the Norwegian ranks to reach the Norwegian commander, but he is not ready to do so where killing is unsanctioned by duty.

For Lady Macbeth, however, greatness consists of being above consideration for the scruples of the general run of men. Ambition, and with it the will-power to gain one's goal, is the highest virtue. "Milk o' human kindness," as far as she is concerned, is a contemptuous allusion to the proverb that milk is a food for infants while meat is the food for men. To have too much of the milk of human kindness is to be what we would call a milksop. Similarly, Lady Macbeth is scornful of the desire to act "holily" (21), like a saint incapable of living in the real world of men.

LINES 30-54

"No compunctious visitings of nature" (45) are to prevent her from doing what she has to do. Here as elsewhere the word "nature" is significant. It implies that the feeling of pity is instinctive. Lady Macbeth is aware that she has the capacity for pity, and this is why she is impelled to call upon evil spirits. She is not a monster; she only wants to become one.

She asks the spirits attendant upon murder to take the milk from her breasts and substitute gall. "Milk" here, as in "milk o' human kindness" and throughout the play, signifies the sweet, gentle qualities of human nature, and gall signifies black, bitter inhuman cruelty. Yet, although compassion is shown to be natural, evil, which disregards all compassion, is omnipresent in the world of *Macbeth*. Paradoxically, although present throughout nature, it is monstrous and unnatural. Although it is immediately and intuitively perceived as contrary to nature, it comes unbidden into men's thoughts, as it did in Macbeth's. "Mortal thoughts" may thus mean not only thoughts which are deadly but thoughts which are mortal because they are characteristic of mortal men, who are prone to sin.

Lady Macbeth concludes her soliloquy by invoking night. Night is to come with a blackness so "thick" (50), so deep, that Heaven will not be able to "peep," as with the eye of a single star, through the "blanket" in which it is enshrouded. This parallels Macbeth's previous calling upon the stars to hide their light. Macbeth had wanted that "the eye wink upon the hand," but Lady Macbeth desires that even the knife itself should not see the wound it makes.

The words "knife," "pall," "dark," and "hell" were closely associated with each other in many passages in Elizabethan literature dealing with the stage. When tragedy was to be performed, the stage was hung with black and the stars represented on the roof of the stage ("the heavens") were blotted out. "Blanket," in addition to the pall in which the figure of tragedy was traditionally represented as enshrouded, suggests a sleeping world, oblivious to the workings of evil. The "murthering ministers" are "sightless," that is, invisible. Evil is present everywhere although unseen, but its deepest affinity is towards the blackness of night. The passage grows out of a traditional concept of tragedy as concerned with affrighting evil, darkness, and hell.

LINES 54-73

Lady Macbeth is as if possessed. Indeed, Elizabethans would have believed that she was literally possessed by the evil spirits whom she had summoned. She greets the entering Macbeth (54-55) by his two present titles and, without naming it, by his title of the future. The threefold greeting and the "all hail" echo the greeting of Macbeth by the witches. She has been "transported" (56), she says, swept forward in time as in a vision beyond "this ignorant present," the present which is ignorant of the future. As was true of Macbeth, she feels her vision of the future to be intensely real. Whereas Macbeth, however, had recoiled with horror from his vision of his murder of Duncan, she speaks with exultation. Her vision of Macbeth as king proves indeed to be real, but in another sense it proves to be a deceitful appearance. Instead of the kingship's bringing them supreme joy, it brings them the utmost torment.

For Lady Macbeth at this moment, however, the murder of Duncan is "this night's great business" (67); it is a heroic enterprise "which shall to all our nights and days to come/Give solely sovereign sway and masterdom" (69-70). The sonorousness of the last line, with its alliterative *s*'s calling to be heavily emphasized and its culmination in the triumphant "masterdom," is expressive of her elation over their future monarchical power. But human beings, particularly those in the grip of evil, are deceived concerning the future. Macbeth's and Lady Macbeth's days— and even more, their nights—are to be given over to anguished restlessness, not the satisfaction of the exercise of power.

The only power Lady Macbeth is to exercise is that over her husband at this very moment and in Scene 7. Carried away with herself, she assumes mastery for the time being over her husband, telling him that she will take care of everything. Murder is unspecified but understood between them.

In referring to it, she makes use of word-play that conveys in its grim humor her half-suppressed exultation. Her lines imply that she will "take care of" Duncan in a different way from their obvious meaning, through murder, and it will be done with "dispatch" ("efficient quickness and speed").

ACT I • SCENE 6

Summary
Duncan on his arrival finds Macbeth's castle to be pleasantly situated. He greets Lady Macbeth, who has come to receive him, and inquires about Macbeth. "I appreciate the love which attends me," Duncan says playfully, "even though it is sometimes a nuisance. In the same way you should be grateful for my love, as shown by this visit, even though it has put you to an inconvenience. You should accordingly pray to God to reward me for this troublesome favor." Lady Macbeth gives the proper reply: "We are devoted to the prayers you ask of us."

Commentary
LINES 1-10
Duncan's remarks about the pleasantness of the atmosphere surrounding the castle where he is to be murdered are dramatically ironic. Banquo's reply (3-10) contains words and images of love and procreation ("loved," "wooingly," "bed," "procreant cradle," "breed") together with those of religious associations ("temple-haunting," "heaven's breath"). The suggestion is that the castle, placed in the midst of nature, is a place of the natural feelings that tie men together—love, devotion, reverence. Banquo too is ironically mistaken. The castle is a place of unnatural evil. The croak of the raven, a bird of ill omen, to which Lady Macbeth refers on hearing the news of Duncan's coming (Act I, Sc. 5, 38-40), more appropriately suggests its atmosphere.

There is probably an implied comparison between Duncan and Christ in the exchange between the King and Lady Macbeth. Such comparisons were frequently made use of in Elizabethan literature to illustrate the idea that the best conduct is that which is most imitative of Christ. Christ was represented as the supreme example of love in his giving himself up for mankind, of whom he asked nothing more than that it love him in return, as Duncan asks Lady Macbeth to do and as she falsely states she will do. Lady Macbeth adds that everything that Macbeth and she possess is really Duncan's, to be accounted for whenever he wishes. Her words are a ceremonious statement of feudal vassalage, but "compt" was frequently used to refer to the accounting at the Day of Judgment, and the statement may have a further meaning, of which she is unaware: Macbeth and she are disregarding their debt to Christ, to whom mankind owes everything, and are forgetful of the great reckoning to be held at their death.

ACT I • SCENE 7

Summary

Macbeth, overcome by his thoughts, has left the banquet hall before the ceremonial supper for Duncan is over. Alone, he gives voice to his feeling concerning the rashness and the awfulness of the projected murder. He gives three reasons for not performing the murder, in the order of ascending climax: it would be imprudent; it would violate the blood-tie of a kinsman, the allegiance of a subject, and the duty of a host; and Duncan has been so blameless a king that to kill him would be monstrous. The culmination of Macbeth's speech is a visualization of the entire world weeping for his victim. Lady Macbeth, worried by his absence, enters and reproaches him for having left the chamber. When Macbeth tells her that they will not go through with the murder, she accuses him of not loving her and of lacking manhood. She goes on to say that she has known the tenderness of nursing a child, but if she had sworn as he had done to perform the deed she would have dashed the baby's brains out before she violated her oath. Her words show that she is not without womanly feelings, for she has experienced a mother's love, but she violently suppresses these feelings and implicitly calls upon Macbeth to suppress compassion, "the milk o' human kindness," as unworthy of a man. She prevails over him, and he admiringly exclaims that her spirit is such that she should bear only boys. They cannot fail, she adds, if they summon up enough courage. Duncan will be sound asleep as a result of his hard day's riding, and she will see to it that his two grooms of the bed-chamber will have been so plied with liquor that they will be in a drunken sleep. He exclaims in admiration of her and proposes that they use the daggers of the two men and smear the men themselves with blood so that suspicion will fall on them. She agrees, and host and hostess return to their royal guest with smiling faces of hospitality.

Commentary
LINES 1-28

In his opening statement concerning the imprudence of the murder, Macbeth says that if he could be sure of the consequences here on earth he would take a chance on the next world. His very phrasing of the idea indicates the desperate courage with which, lured by a great attraction, he regards the risk. Life is conceived of as a bank or sandbar on the verge of being covered by the ocean of eternity, and the risk of an after-life is a frantic leap into the unknown. Later, when Macbeth speaks of Duncan's virtues, however, he refers definitely to the "deep damnation" (20) entailed for the murderer.

The irony is that he is right in both instances. He will get the retribution here on earth of which he speaks, his own actions and words turning against him. As one of his nobles says at the conclusion (Act V, Sc.3, 18), the revolts springing up all about him will remind him of his own breach of faith in murdering Duncan. He will also be aware that he has given up his immortal soul to Satan (Act III, Sc. 1, 67-68). It would have been well if Macbeth had paid heed to his own words instead of accepting the philosophy that the extraordinary man can make his own law and his own future, secure against the consequences of his violation of natural law. The theme of the future, its relation to the present, to one's actions, to the possibility of foreseeing it through supernatural aid or intuition, is one of the main themes of the play. Macbeth here foresees it accurately, as Lady Macbeth had not.

LINES 28-83

Another important theme is the theme of what constitutes a true man. It is here introduced in the dramatic exchange between Macbeth and his wife. To her taunt of cowardice, he replies in effect (46-47) that murder is inhuman and not a sign of manliness. Lady Macbeth replies that he was a man when he suggested the idea of murder and that if he would only do now what he had before dared to talk about, he would be even more of a man. The great opportunity which has come to him has only acted to "unmake" (54) him, to undo his manhood. That Lady Macbeth has a man's spirit, not a woman's, her husband regards as praiseworthy. He does not realize that in having called upon the spirits of evil to unsex her (Act I, Sc. 5, 40-41) she has become evil and unnatural, just as she is demanding that he become evil and unnatural.

Nevertheless it takes a tremendous effort of the will for him to act in accordance with the concept of what it is to be a true man which he has taken for his own. Macbeth has to exert every power to make every organ of his body obey his will (80-81), for that which he is about to do is so unnatural that there is an internal rebellion within him.

The relation between Macbeth and his wife in this scene is also unnatural, as the Elizabethans would have conceived it. The function of a husband was to rule his family but to rule in love and in reason, as the king

32

rules over his subjects. For the wife to rule is unnatural. Lady Macbeth does not address herself to her husband's reason but to his passions, which should be commanded by his reason—to his pride and to his ambition. She is also implicitly calling upon him to put his love for her before his love for God. In doing so, she is, unthinking of the momentousness of the deed and of the consequences it will have for them and their entire people, like Eve tempting Adam to share her fall. History repeats itself because as a result of the fall of Adam men are prone to sin and consequently constantly repeat the pattern Adam set. We need not accept either the Elizabethans' view of women or their theology to respond to the power of the scene which these overtones help to give it or to perceive that Lady Macbeth is making use of two traditional and powerful wifely weapons: "You don't really love me" and "You are not a man."

ACT II • SCENE 1

Summary

In a court within the castle Banquo and his son Fleance are walking about. Banquo is disturbed and cannot sleep. He is momentarily startled when he hears someone but relaxes when he finds that it is Macbeth. He tells Macbeth that he dreamt last night of the three witches, but Macbeth pretends that they have been absent from his thoughts. They agree to discuss the significance of the encounter at some other time. When Macbeth speaks vaguely of Banquo's supporting him at the proper time, promising to reward him if he does so, Banquo replies that he will if he can in so doing maintain his blamelessness and his true allegiance to the king.

Macbeth, left alone, awaits the sound of the bell which is to be the signal that the preparations for the murder of Duncan have been completed. As he waits, it seems to him that there before him is an air-borne dagger that moves towards Duncan's bed-chamber and, as he looks upon it, becomes covered with blood. Awful visions fill his mind. The bell sounds, and he proceeds measuredly and stealthily up the staircase leading to Duncan's chamber.

Commentary

LINES 1-32

Banquo is unable to sleep because the powers of evil are seeking to work upon him. It is after midnight—the witching hour—and there are no stars in the darkness (4-5), as Macbeth had previously wished. Until the last act, when there is a restoration of light, the scenes are predominantly to be set in darkness. The "fog and filthy air" of the witches—the obscuration of daylight—has been succeeded by pitch blackness.

Banquo continues to be a contrast to Macbeth. He too is visited by temptation, but he calls upon heaven to help him to resist "the cursèd thoughts that nature/ Gives way to in repose!" (8-9). Human nature gives way to evil dreams in sleep because evil is in human nature as well as all around it. However, also in human nature is reason, which enables us to control our evil impulses. In this world of evil we cannot afford to relax our resistance to it for a moment. But Banquo is staunchly loyal to the king. While Macbeth uses "honour" (25) to mean distinction, Banquo uses it to mean the merit that deserves such distinction, without which such distinction is false.

The inception of this encounter between the true thane and the false thane is dramatically ironic: Banquo, who has given his sword to Fleance, acting as his squire, calls for it when, tense as he is, he hears a sound. He is reassured when he sees that the noise was made by his host—but his first impulse was right.

LINES 33-64

The vision of the dagger illustrates once more the power of Macbeth's imagination. It is also another playing upon the theme of the difference between appearance and reality. It recedes from him as he seeks to grasp it, leading him in the direction of Duncan's room. It seems as real as his own dagger, which he now draws, but he cannot touch it. Are his eyes deluded while his other senses are true—another instance of the conflict between Macbeth's senses—or do they perceive something which has a reality unapprehended by his other senses?

Macbeth addresses the dagger floating in the air as "fatal vision" (36). It is a vision showing what seems to him to have been sent by fate to lead him to the sleeping Duncan, a vision that will be fatal to Duncan. Macbeth is as if in the grip of the future. He follows the dagger as if he were a sleep-walker moving without his volition. The hour is one in which over the entire hemisphere "Nature seems dead, and wicked dreams abuse/ The curtained sleep." There is no sound or motion. Everything seems to be dead. Only evil dreams which deceive the sleepers seem to be real, and he himself seems to be in such a dream as he "moves" with "stealthy pace" "like a ghost" (54-56). In the awful silence he looks upon himself as if he were disengaged from his own body, a spirit looking upon a body proceeding towards its awful task as if it were walking in a dream. The sound of the bell—one of the many effective noises either heard off-stage or suggested in the imagery during the action immediately before, during, and after the murder—breaks the silence and rouses him to perform his terrible deed.

ACT II • SCENE 2

Summary

Lady Macbeth is waiting tensely for her husband to commit the murder. Keyed up, she hears the owl's shriek, which was supposed to portend death and which she hence compares to the bellman or town-crier who was sent to toll his bell in front of the prison on the night of the execution of a condemned criminal. She envisages Macbeth killing Duncan. She would have killed him herself, she reveals with a humanizing touch, if he had not resembled her father as he slept. There is a cry from outside the room, and she is for a moment afraid that the two grooms have awaked and the attempt has been unsuccessful. Nothing happens, however, and after a few instants Macbeth enters. After having committed the murder, he passed a room in which a man, roused from his sleep by a dream, called out "Murder!" awakening his companion. It was Donalbain, one of the king's sons, and his attendant. Macbeth had to stand outside of the door waiting for them to go to sleep again before he could continue. One of them cried "God bless us!" but Macbeth could not give the automatic reply to a blessing, for the word "Amen" stuck in his throat. It seemed to him that he heard a voice proclaiming that, since he had murdered sleep, he would sleep no more. Lady Macbeth urges him to come to himself and to wash the blood off his hands. Noticing the daggers in his hands, she asks him why has he brought them and tells him to take them back and smear the faces of the drugged grooms with blood. He cannot bring himself to return, and she goes to perform the task. A knocking at the gate startles Macbeth, and he wishes that it could rouse Duncan, but time cannot be rolled back. On Lady Macbeth's return, the knocking continuing, she hurries him off to get the blood off his hands and to change into a dressing-gown. It must seem as if they have been roused from sleep.

Commentary
LINES 1-14

The murder takes place off-stage. The sight of Duncan being killed would have alienated our sympathy from Macbeth and Lady Macbeth. We have to see through their eyes and to hear through their ears in order to share their terror and horror.

LINES 14-56

The strange sounds off-stage alternate with tense silences. Macbeth never answers Lady Macbeth's question (16), first replying with a number of questions indicative of his confusion and then, distracted by an imaginary noise, which causes him to listen strainedly, forgetting it and addressing her with another question of his own. It was he, having thought he heard a voice, whom she had heard call out. The cross-questions suggest their extreme tension.

Lady Macbeth's unimaginative practicality and her skeptical rationalism contrast with Macbeth's visionary imagination. When he tells her of the voice that had three times said he would sleep no more (41-42), the three forms of address echoing the witches' greetings of him, she asks "Who was it that thus cried," as if it could only have been the voice of an identifiable person. For her Macbeth's dwelling on what he has heard is simply thinking "brainsickly" (45), a contemptuous synonym for "insanely." She says in a dramatically ironic foreshadowing of her eventual mental collapse that such thoughts will make them mad. She is not afraid to go back to plant the daggers by the drugged grooms and the dead Duncan: "The sleeping, and the dead,/ Are but as pictures; 'Tis the eye of childhood/ That fears a painted devil" (53-54). In other words, she is saying: "Don't be a child; be a man," as though manhood consists of being superior to conscience and religious dreads.

Macbeth, looking upon his "hangsman's hands" (27)—hangsmen had such tasks as disemboweling living persons—refers to his wife's telling him to wash "this filthy witness" (46) off his hands. For her the blood is merely evidence to be got rid of, physically repulsive, but nothing more. For him it is symbolic of his guilt, which he can never get rid of. The entire ocean will not wash his hand clean. As he horrifiedly regards his hand, he imagines its red slowly turning the green of the ocean to crimson. This celebrated image is the most powerful of the blood images, as his statement that his hands will "pluck out mine eyes" (58) is the most powerful of the images of conflict between parts of the body.

Macbeth's fascinated contemplation of his hands is treated contemptuously by Lady Macbeth, who has returned with bloody hands of her own. "A little water clears us of this deed" (66), she tells him in words that are perhaps reminiscent of Pontius Pilate. She urges him not to be lost in this thought "so poorly," that is, in such a poor-spirited way, and he, rousing himself, replies that it would be better for him to be unconscious forever rather than to have to be continually conscious of his crime.

ACT II • SCENE 3

Summary
A porter, who has been carousing during the night, goes to open the gate at which there is a knocking. He grumbles as he goes to answer the insistent summons and, the thought occurring to him that the porter at hell-gate must be even busier than he, he indulges in a whimsical pretense of being that porter, making believe that he is admitting various sinners. Finally, he admits the noblemen Macduff and Lennox. Macduff has been asked by Duncan to call upon him early in the morning. Macbeth enters in his dressing-gown to greet them. He stands talking to Lennox as Macduff goes to wake the king. Lennox asks whether the king is leaving that day. "He does," replies Macbeth, but corrects himself guiltily. "He did appoint so." Lennox then passes the time, as people do in such circumstances, by talking of the weather. Lennox's talk, however, is not ordinary chit-chat. In his whole life, he says, he has never experienced such a night. Nature was profoundly disturbed. Chimneys were blown down, the earth seemed to shake, there were continuous owl-screechings and strange screams. Such unnatural happenings were supposed to accompany the death of kings. Macbeth, however, merely replies with constrained understatement: "'Twas a rough night." Macduff returns crying out in horror, and Macbeth and Lennox hasten to Duncan's room while Macduff orders the alarm-bell to be rung. Lady Macbeth, Banquo, and Malcolm and Donalbain rush in one after another, and Macbeth and Lennox return. In the midst of the

expressions of horror and dismay, Macbeth tells the company that, carried away by rage at the evidently guilty grooms, he killed them. Lady Macbeth faints and is carried away. The members of the company agree to return to their rooms to get dressed and then to meet to inquire further into the crime. Malcolm and Donalbain remain. They express their fear and suspicion of their kinsmen and decide that it would be safest for them if each were to flee to a different haven, Malcolm to England and Donalbain to Ireland.

Commentary
LINES 1-43

The comic interlude of the porter serves a number of purposes. It is dramatically necessary to fill the interval while Macbeth and Lady Macbeth go to change their clothes. The contrast between the porter's bleary-eyed grumbling return to his normal workaday routine after a night's carousing and the pretense of Macbeth of awakening to ordinary, everyday reality after his unknown night of horror is ironic. Even more ironic is the fact that the porter's whimsy of being keeper of hell-gate is more true than he realizes: it is indeed a hell into which the castle of Macbeth has been transformed by his awful deed. In bringing us back to the normal world, the porter makes us realize this more sharply. His jesting acts as a relief from extreme tension, but it is thematically significant.

When the knocking at the gate had first started, it had appalled Macbeth, not because he had feared being detected but because it seemed, like the other sounds and voices he had heard, terrifyingly ominous. Indeed it was. Macbeth did not know it, but the person doing the knocking was Macduff, who has been born to kill him. The knocking was as the sound of fate. With the entrance of the porter the knocking, which had given such urgency to the action of Lady Macbeth in the scene before, becomes the signal of the return to normality. With the coming of day, life is re-commencing and resuming its natural course.

But normality is always followed by new abnormalities. Life at all times is subject to the promptings of evil. The porter's jokes about the familiar things of the day would have universalized the murder for the Elizabethans. His admission to hell of the "equivocator" is a grimly ironic reference to the very recent Gunpowder Plot, which had shocked England greatly. Some of the participants in this conspiracy were Jesuits, who adhered to the doctrine that under duress one may swear to statements made with mental reservations or deceptive ambiguities. The porter's comment would therefore have linked this would-be treasonable murder with that of the distant past being enacted on the stage and suggested that the struggle with evil goes on everlastingly. Macbeth, it should be noted, having falsely played the part of a welcoming host, has from now on to deceive, to utter words which he does not mean, but he too cannot equivocate to heaven. He himself will be deceived by the witches, of whose "equivocation" (Act V, Sc. 5, 43) he is to learn when he finds that their words of seeming reassurance have another meaning.

LINES 44-64

The conversation that Macbeth engages in before the discovery of the murder is loaded with dramatic irony. He is addressed by conventional titles of courtesy—"noble Sir" (44) and "worthy Thane" (46)—but in the circumstances these serve as a comment on what Macbeth has done: it was ignoble, not noble, and anything but worthy of a thane toward his king. Beneath the exchange with Macduff are similar ironies.

LINES 64-96

Macduff, like Macbeth, but for different reasons, finds the sight of the dead Duncan too terrible to look upon. It is "the great doom's image" (79), a sight as awful as the Day of Judgment. Duncan's death is a prefiguration of the time of universal death, as the sleep from which Macduff is calling Malcolm, Donalbain, and Banquo to rouse themselves, is "death's counterfeit" (77).

Everyone is aroused by the clanging of the alarm-bell, used in the times of direst emergencies to summon men to arms. To Lady Macbeth's question as to the reason for the summons, Macduff, addressing her as "gentle lady," says that it is not for a woman to hear (84-86). The words are doubly ironic in view of her call to be unsexed and Macbeth's praise of her masculine courage.

Macbeth's profession of grief is also dramatically ironic. If he had died an hour before Duncan, he says (91-96), he would have lived a happy life, but from now on there is nothing worthwhile left. This is not merely a lament for Duncan, expressed in conventional terms, which Macbeth delivers in continuing to play his part, although it is that. It also has a significance of which the others are unaware, expressing his overwhelming consciousness of sin.

LINES 97-146

Lady Macbeth's swoon, sometimes thought to be pretended, is probably genuine. She screwed her courage to the sticking-point, but now that everything has gone through as planned, she relaxes the tension of her will and collapses.

ACT II • SCENE 4

Summary

An old man and Ross, standing outside Macbeth's castle, discuss the strange natural phenomena that have taken place. Macduff enters and gives them the latest news. It has been decided that the two grooms killed Duncan, and, since Malcolm and Donalbain ran away, apparently because of guilty fear, it is believed that the grooms were in their pay. Macbeth has been chosen king and is to be crowned at Scone. Macduff, who is not going to the coronation, expresses uneasiness about the future.

Commentary

LINES 1-20

The unnamed old man is a person of rank and dignity who has seen many strange things in his life and has the wisdom of age. He acts as a choric commentator. His conversation with Ross points up the strangeness of recent events. The word "strange," used by the old man (3) and reiterated by Ross (14), signifies the unnatural. It occurs frequently in the course of the play.

Ross asks (8-10) whether the darkness in mid-day they are experiencing is caused by Night's having gained the ascendancy over Day or by Day's hiding itself in shame over the guilt of man. The antithesis between day and night, here as elsewhere, is linked up with the antithesis between good and evil and that between order and chaos. Has evil triumphed, or is good only temporarily in abeyance? Are we witnessing the end of things?

The idea of the possible end of things is suggested more strongly in Ross's immediately preceding words (5-6): "Thou seest the heavens, as troubled with man's act,/ Threatens his bloody stage." This makes use of the common idea of the time that the world is a stage, with man the actor in a play and God the spectator. It suggests that God is looking on and shows his anger by the eclipse, which is a threat of the coming of the Day of Judgment. "Heavens" is not merely a synonym for God; it has a theatrical meaning. In the Elizabethan theater the roof of the stage, bespangled with stars, was called the "heavens." "Act" similarly means primarily "deed," but it also refers to the division of a play. It is noteworthy also that the Elizabethan stage was draped with black when a tragedy was being shown. The theatrical terms have the effect of universalizing the evil committed by Macbeth: what the audience is witnessing as it watches the tragedy of *Macbeth*—and the audience is reminded that it is watching a stage representation by the imagery and diction—is the tragedy of mankind itself.

LINES 20-41

The terseness with which Macduff replies to Ross in giving the "official" theory of the crime indicates some holding back in accepting it. It was Macduff, it will be remembered, who in the previous scene asked Macbeth why he killed the grooms. In telling Ross that he will not attend the coronation, he expresses the hope that the coronation will really be for the good of the country. He does not have any definite suspicions, but he is uneasy.

The old man's couplet, which concludes the scene, is spoken with something of a seer's vision. Uttered to himself as Macduff and Ross have turned to leave, he calls down a blessing on those persons who, not knowing where evil lies, are ready to accept as friends those who mean no good. The words act as a warning of things to come, but they are also an assurance that good, though deceived by evil, will finally triumph.

ACT III • SCENE 1

Summary

Banquo comments that all of the predictions of the witches have proved true for Macbeth but that he fears that Macbeth has engaged in foul play to make this so. Nevertheless, since they prophesied that he will be the father of kings, he has reason to hope. Just then, the trumpets announce the coming of Macbeth, now king, and his court. Macbeth reminds Banquo of that evening's feast, at which Banquo is to be the chief guest. While paying compliments to Banquo and talking to him about a council meeting to be held the next day, Macbeth slips in three questions: "Ride you this afternoon?", "Is't far you ride?", and "Goes Fleance with you?" These are what he is really concerned with in the conversation. We learn of their significance a little later. Dismissing his court, Macbeth sends for two men who are waiting outside the palace gate at his command. While he is waiting for them to arrive, Macbeth expresses in soliloquy his fear of Banquo, whose valor and ability promise that the witches' prophecy concerning him will be fulfilled. If so, Macbeth will have incurred damnation only for the descendants of Banquo. The murderers entering, Macbeth reminds them of a previous conversation in which he had explained to them that it was Banquo who had been the cause of troubles which had befallen them. He asks them if they are ready to let their wrongs go by unavenged, and, on being assured that they are not, informs them that Banquo is also his enemy. They can both avenge themselves and gain his favor by waylaying Banquo and his son Fleance. He will send word to them within an hour as to where to station themselves.

Commentary
LINES 1-46

Banquo has been thought by some critics to be acquiescing here in Macbeth's accession and becoming an accessory to the murder after the fact as a result of ambition. It is doubtful, however, that Shakespeare would have portrayed James I's ancestor thus unfavorably. Banquo suspects Macbeth, but there is nothing that he can do at the moment. In fact, it is uncertain that there is anything that he could properly do, since in the officially promulgated political theory, it was sinful to conspire or rebel against any king, even one who had ascended the throne wrongly. The insurrection against Macbeth at the end is an exception, so horrible are Macbeth's crimes, but at this moment Macbeth has not yet proved himself an absolute tyrant. Ambition would have caused Banquo to proceed against Macbeth, as Macbeth had proceeded against Duncan, to try to realize the witches' prophecy. He is, however, content to bide his time, secure in the belief that the future is governed by God's plan, which will work itself out.

LINES 47-71

Macbeth had regarded the kingship as the height of human desire.

Ironcially, however, he finds no pleasure in it. He now thinks that if only he can get rid of Banquo, he will rest secure, but this is only a self-delusion, for his fears multiply. Macbeth will never feel secure, for he knows that the crown is not rightfully his. He lives in the knowledge that he has killed a king and fears that he has taught others a lesson in doing so. Despairing of the next world, he devotes himself entirely to securing his safety in this world. From now on, he is resolute in seeking this end.

In speaking of his fears of Banquo, Macbeth pays him an involuntary tribute. Banquo, he says, is of a regal nature and is both courageous and prudent. We remember the soliloquy in which Macbeth told himself that it would be imprudent as well as immoral to kill Duncan. Banquo is neither.

In his expression of disillusionment Macbeth uses images of infertility: he has acquired a "fruitless crown" (60) and a "barren sceptre" (61). This is appropriate, for evil is destructive and sterile rather than creative and life-giving. Since Lady Macbeth, in giving herself to evil, had asked to be unsexed, Macbeth cannot be "father to a line of kings" (59).

In referring to Banquo, however, Macbeth makes use of an image of fertility: the "seed of Banquo" will be kings (69). So Banquo in his soliloquy had said that the witches had stated that he would be the "root and father/ Of many kings" (5-6). In previous scenes (Act I, Sc. 4 and 6), Banquo has also employed images of fertility. The opposition between Macbeth and Banquo, between the unnatural and the natural, the sterile and the fertile, continues throughout. Rather than accept the idea of Banquo's being father to a line of kings, Macbeth tries to fight against the future.

LINES 72-141

The two men to whom Macbeth speaks are not professional murderers, as are the brutal hirelings whom Macbeth later employs to kill Lady Macduff and her son. They are ruined gentlemen who in their desperation are ready to do anything. They had thought their troubles came from Macbeth, as we are to suppose that in fact they did, but he has convinced them that they come from Banquo. Once again, we have the impression of the inability of men to distinguish the evil from the good.

Macbeth employs with them arguments similar to those which Lady Macbeth had employed with him. If they are "not i' th' worst rank of manhood" (102), he tells them, they will revenge themselves on Banquo. The implication is that there is an order of manliness and that revengeful murderers stand in the front ranks of this order. "Bounteous nature" (97) has established such an order among men, as she has among dogs. But the order of which Macbeth speaks is a reversal of natural order, and the concept of manhood contained in it is a false concept.

With the same scorn that Lady Macbeth showed in disposing of his moral objections he sweeps aside the idea of Christian forgiveness and of the acceptance of the world's misfortunes as God's will. The first ruined gentleman, speaking for both, accepts the view that men with the passions of men and not the spiritlessness of milksops will take revenge.

ACT III • SCENE 2

Summary

Lady Macbeth shares her husband's sense of insecurity and his fear of Banquo. The scene begins as the previous one had ended, with the word "Banquo." The servant's statement to her that Banquo will return that night underscores the irony of Banquo's previous assurance to that effect: although dead, Banquo will indeed return that night in a form that will be more frightening to Macbeth than ever. The conversation between Macbeth and his wife reveals a change of relationship between them. Macbeth addresses her as lovingly as before, but he has taken charge and plotted on his own to kill Banquo. He hints of it to Lady Macbeth but does not divulge it to her. She, in turn, no longer addresses him scornfully but tries to comfort his tortured mind. In a weak repetition of her previous advice she hints that Banquo and Fleance are mortal and can therefore be killed and urges him not to reveal his thoughts in his face and his manner at the supper that night. In a similar repetition of his previous apostrophe to Night, Macbeth calls upon it to sew up "the tender eye of pitiful Day" (46-47), as the eyes of falcons were sewn up to deprive them of sight and make them tractable, and with its "bloody and invisible hand" (48) to tear up the bond between fate and Banquo. As if in response to his summons, night begins to fall, and Macbeth looking out upon it again imagines all of nature falling asleep while "Night's black agents" rouse themselves once more.

Commentary

Although Macbeth and his wife seem superficially to have been drawn closer together by the crime in which they have participated, we see the beginnings of an alienation between them. She asks him why he stays by himself, making as his companions his miserable thoughts and imaginings (8-9). Alienated from mankind by his crime, Macbeth is to be increasingly alienated from his wife. He lives alone in his tormented inner world, of which his images of torture (he refers to a mental torture rack in lines 21-22 and says on line 36 that his mind is "full of scorpions," swarming and stinging) give indication. She in her turn, after expressing her fear of Banquo, feels it imperative on his entrance to hide her anxiety.

Both Lady Macbeth and Macbeth express envy of Duncan in his grave. Macbeth underscores the irony. To gain peace, he has sent Duncan to his peace while he lies in torment on his sleepless bed. Life for Macbeth is a "fitful fever" (33), from which there is rest only in death. In another disease image he speaks of the "affliction" of his "terrible dreams," which "shake" him nightly (17-19). The prophecy of the voice which cried that he would sleep no more has been fulfilled.

Macbeth is suffering a poetically appropriate retribution. He killed the sleeping Duncan; therefore, he cannot sleep. He feasted Duncan before killing him; therefore, he is condemned to "eat our meal in fear" (17). He has played the hypocritical host, and he must continue to do so, dissimulating despite his internal torment at the ceremonial supper he is about to hold. In an image of universal disorder (16) Macbeth states that he would rather that the world fell to pieces, indeed that both heaven and earth be destroyed, than that he continue to suffer as he does.

ACT III • SCENE 3

Summary
The two murderers have been joined by a third, sent by Macbeth. They await the coming of Banquo and Fleance in a park that has a road leading to the palace. Banquo and Fleance dismount off-stage and come walking along the road. The murderers dash out of the torch and kill Banquo, but Fleance gets away in the darkness.

Commentary
The third murderer has been sent by Macbeth, who has a tyrant's distrust of his agents. The two murderers were at first suspicious of the newcomer, but he has convinced them by repeating the preliminary instruction Macbeth has given them. In the world of evil no one can be sure of anyone.

Because it is evil, the world of *Macbeth* is a world of danger. The belated traveller spurs to get to the inn before nightfall because it is dangerous to ride abroad at night. So does Banquo, the last of the guests to arrive for the supper. The palace is, however, no harbor for him. Less than a mile from it he is killed.

Banquo's conversational remark about the weather—"It will rain tonight" (16)—indicates that he is unprepared and that the night is starless, a fit night for murder. The grimly humorous comment on this remark by the first murderer—"Let it come down"—as they rain a storm of blows at him indicates the fierce delight with which they take a supposed revenge. The solicitude of the dying Banquo for his son, as he urges him to escape, contrasts with their ferocity.

ACT III • SCENE 4

Summary
The guests are assembled for the banquet. Macbeth leaves for a moment to speak to the first murderer at the door. He is elated by the news of Banquo's death, but his elation is dashed when he learns that Fleance has escaped. Returning to the feast, he resumes his role as gracious host and expresses his regret at the absence of Banquo. At this moment he sees the ghost of Banquo seated in his own place at the head of the table. He speaks wildly to it, and Lady Macbeth expostulates with him. Lady Macbeth in urging Macbeth to regain his self-command at this crucial moment makes use of her previous arguments and her previous scornful tone. She speaks as a disbeliever in the supernatural: it's only his imagination. His conduct is unbecoming a man, she asserts. It is folly that unmans him because what he sees can only be a delusion derived from the womanish credulity that

accepts old wives' tales. The ghost disappears, and Macbeth momentarily recovers himself. When Macbeth, however, again states his wish that Banquo were here, the ghost reappears. Macbeth confronts it with words similar to those he had used in defending himself against his wife when they were discussing the murder of Duncan: "What man dare, I dare" (98). He raves on wildly, and the ghost once more disappears. This time, however, the guests cannot contain their agitation, and when Ross addresses a question to Macbeth, Lady Macbeth hurriedly dismisses them. Macbeth, left alone with Lady Macbeth, voices his horror, but then he determinedly recovers his self-control and turns to something concrete: the danger which Macduff, who has refused to come to the feast, poses. He announces his purpose of repairing to the witches to learn more of what awaits him in the future and of continuing in his way of crime in his effort to render himself secure.

Commentary
LINES 1-31

Each of the first three speeches of Macbeth and Lady Macbeth ends with the word "welcome." Everything is done in proper ceremonial manner. Macbeth invites the nobles to seat themselves according to their degrees. Order is being observed—but it is soon to be broken. When Lady Macbeth dismisses the company, she says (118), "Stand not upon the order of your going."

Speaking to the murderer, Macbeth is elatedly jocular. When he hears, however, that Fleance has escaped, he finds the fever which Fleance's death was supposed to cure returning again. He comments that if Fleance would have been killed, he would have been in perfect health. Macbeth thus continually deludes himself: one more murder, and everything will be well. Nevertheless he momentarily reassures himself with the thought that, regardless of the future, Fleance is no danger at present.

LINES 31-120

The ghost of Banquo is not an hallucination. Ghosts were thought to have the power to render themselves visible only to the person whom they wished to see them. That this ghost was intended to be real is indicated by the stage direction concerning its appearance in the original text. A ghost having existence only in Macbeth's fevered imagination would not have been given bodily form.

LINES 121-143

Lady Macbeth's brief replies to Macbeth indicate that, the crisis past, she is overcome by fatigue as a result of the strain. Macbeth, after brooding for a moment over thoughts of supernatural retribution, abruptly comes to himself, signalling his return to the here and now by asking her what time it is. He is determined to continue along his way. He cannot return to the past, he says in his image of wading in blood (135-137), but must attain his goal of security through more crime and more blood. Further crime, he thinks, will harden him against fear and obliterate the horrible visions which by the conclusion of the scene he has come to believe are imagined by him. The last line signifies that he will cease to be a fearful novice with childish terrors and will become mature, a man, in crime.

At the very time in which Macbeth expresses his determination to perpetrate new crimes, however, there is a hint of the first streaks of a new dawn. Mention of Macduff carries an unconscious symbolic significance, for it is he who is to bring about the dawn, immediately afterwards.

ACT III • SCENE 5

Summary
Hecate rebukes the witches for having dealt with Macbeth without calling upon her. She will distill a vaporous drop on the moon and from it raise false visions which will deceive Macbeth.

Commentary
This scene is a non-Shakespearean interpolation. Including a song written by Thomas Middleton, its iambic meter opposes the trochaic meter of Shakespeare's witches and dispels the atmosphere of foulness and grotesque unnaturalness.

ACT III • SCENE 6

Summary
Lennox speaks ironically to another lord about the official theory that Malcolm and Donalbain had had Duncan killed, saying that no doubt Fleance had done the same with his father Banquo. We are told that Macduff has gone to England, where Malcolm has been received by the British king, Edward the Confessor, to ask that an army be levied against Macbeth.

Commentary
Macbeth, tormented by his conscience but unable to give up the crown and repent, has revealed himself as a tyrant. The people of Scotland cannot eat and sleep in peace (33-35). A king creates a kingdom in his own image, and Macbeth, unable to eat and sleep in quiet, has caused the same to be true of his country. However, we see an opposition developing and a force being assembled in England.

ACT IV • SCENE 1

Summary
The witches, in a dark cave in the middle of which is a boiling cauldron, throw loathsome ingredients into the hellish stew. Hecate and three other witches enter, engage in song, and leave. Macbeth enters and demands to know the answers to his questions. The witches produce an

apparition, an armed head, which anticipates his question and tells him to beware of Macduff. Then they produce a second apparition, a bloody child, which tells him that no man born of woman can harm him. Macbeth, elated, says that to make assurance doubly sure he will nevertheless have Macduff killed. Finally, the witches produce a third apparition, a child crowned with a tree in his hand, who tells him that he will never be vanquished until great Birnam Wood shall come against him to high Dunsinane Hill. Macbeth, still more elated, now demands to know whether Banquo's issue will ever reign. There appears a procession of eight kings, the last with a mirror in his hand, with Banquo, bloody as before, following. In the magic mirror of the eighth king, Macbeth sees many more kings, some with two-fold orbs and treble sceptres. Banquo smilingly points the kings out as his. The witches then mockingly dance about and vanish. Macbeth, dismayed, calls Lennox from where he has been standing guard before the cave to ask him whether he saw them pass. Lennox has not, but he gives Macbeth the news that Macduff has fled to England. Macbeth resolves that from now on he will do immediately whatever terrible thing comes to his mind and begins by deciding to put Lady Macduff and her children to death.

Commentary
LINES 1-47

This scene is a grotesque parody of old women bending over their cooking. They are making a good, thick gruel, but the objects in it are repulsive and unnatural. Hecate's speech is generally believed to be another interpolation from Middleton, as is indicated by the iambic metre and the ineptness of the comparison of Shakespeare's "secret, black, and midnight hags" (48) to "elves and fairies in a ring" (42).

LINES 48-135

Macbeth's conjuration is an invocation of chaos. Though the whole world be destroyed, he wishes that the future be revealed to him. He cares not for the achievements of man: religion, commerce, agriculture, architecture, and present and past civilizations generally ("palaces, and pyramids" [57]). The culmination is his willingness that "Nature's germens tumble all together" (59), that is, that the seeds from which everything in the future is to gain existence be tumbled together in confusion, producing barrenness or monstrosities. These are the same elemental seeds to which Banquo referred when he spoke of "the seeds of time" (Act I, Sc. 3, 58), but Banquo assumed that these seeds would grow in accordance with a divine plan. Here is another contrast between Macbeth the destroyer and Banquo the creator.

The armed head represents Macduff as the soldier whom Macbeth knows him to be and as he will appear, as Macbeth does not know, in the battle in which Macduff is to kill him. The apparition tells Macbeth what he already believes, that he should beware Macduff, just as in Macbeth's first encounter with the witches the first witch, in greeting him as the Thane of Glamis, told him what he already knew.

The bloody child represents Macduff untimely ripped from his mother's womb. Macbeth does not know this but the fact already exists as the fated means of Macbeth's death. This fact corresponds to the greeting of Macbeth as Thane of Cawdor by the second witch, something which was already true but of which he did not have knowledge. But Macbeth hopes to bind fate by killing Macduff, for then fate would have to violate not just one but two of its own laws if Macduff were to destroy Macbeth: the law of birth, that man is born of woman, and the law of death, that dead men cannot regain bodily existence and mortal power.

The child crowned with a tree in his hand represents Malcolm triumphant as king, with the branch of Birnam Wood in his hand which he had ordered his soldiers to carry. This is the event which will take place in the future, of which Macbeth does not know. It is the future which Macbeth seeks to suppress in its babyhood but which inevitably grows to its full power. Macbeth exultantly accepts the apparition's prophecy that he need not fear rebellion, for this implies that he will live the term of life allotted by nature and die of old age. He, who has outraged nature, thinks to die a natural death, but as is indicated by the child with the tree in his hand, nature itself will rise against him.

The witches and the apparitions they summon have throughout refused to elaborate on what they have said, tantalizing Macbeth even as they have voiced their predictions. Now, when Macbeth asks about Banquo's issue, they reply with one voice, "Seek to know no more." It is a sure way to lure him to inquire further. They now show him a spectacle designed to grieve his heart. It is a spectacle that undoubtedly gladdened the heart of Shakespeare's king and appealed to the patriotism of the audience, for James I, who succeeded Elizabeth after having been James VI of Scotland, was supposed to be of the line of Banquo. The kings shown in the magic mirror represent the monarchs who will rule after James over England and Scotland, it is implied, until the end of the world.

The speech of the first witch (125-132) and the dance are probably another interpolation. The speech is in iambic meter, and it would have been more effective for the witches to vanish when he turns to them with the question "What! is this so?" (124). The witches always mockingly leave their beguiled victim unsatisfied.

LINES 135-156

Macbeth's furious exclamation that all those who trust the witches should be damned (139) is a curse that returns upon himself, for after this outburst he does continue to trust them, more and more in desperation. The news that Macduff has fled to England serves in Macbeth's mind to confirm the predictions, for already the warning that he should beware Macuff is proving true. Time, he cries out (144), has forestalled the terrible actions that he was going to perform. In killing Duncan, Macbeth was seeking to speed up time, to make it yield that which had been promised him. Now it seems to him that he is in a race against time. He has to act immediately once an idea comes to his mind lest time deprive him of the opportunity to put it into effect. The sound of galloping horses which he heard (139-140), one of a number of images of rapid riding in the play which contribute to a sense of goaded swiftness, here perhaps suggests the onrush of time as well as the sound of the witches' horses.

The language in which he expresses his resolution to put his thoughts into action immediately is significant. The first purposes his heart may form (147-48) will be the first things his hands will do. Evil is his only firstborn, the only thing he can hatch; otherwise, he is barren. Also, it should be noted that there is now no internal war within him: what his heart wishes, his hand does. But this is at the price of the suppression within himself of his moral sense, which caused his body to revolt against what he thought to do.

Macbeth, despite his sense of time operating against him, is unaware of the forces that are gathering and that will hem him in. Lennox, who has been standing guard and who tells him of Macduff's escape, is, we have seen, secretly sympathetic to Macduff and opposed to Macbeth. This is the last time we see Macbeth together with anyone whom we have previously seen in the play, even Lady Macbeth, until he is killed by Macduff. He is terribly and utterly alone.

ACT IV • SCENE 2

Summary
Lady Macduff is complaining to Ross about her husband's flight, which she considers imprudent and a sign of lack of concern for her and their children. She complains that he must be lacking in the feeling of love for his family natural to all things, for even the wren, the smallest of birds, will fight the owl to protect her young. Ross assures her that Macduff did what was best for him to do. His reply gives us a picture of what Scotland has become under Macbeth. The feverishness and convulsions of the time indicate how the "fitful fever" of Macbeth has spread throughout the kingdom, for a country is healthy only as its ruler is. Like Macbeth, the people are beset with fears, fears that spring from rumors, which in turn originate from fears. In a land dominated by fear, one cannot tell what is true and what is false. The disorder image is reminiscent of the sailor's ship that was tempest-tossed by the witch. After Ross leaves, Lady Macduff and her son engage in some sad joking. A messenger, risking his life by his coming and expressing pity for Lady Macduff and her children, enters to warn her to fly with her children immediately. Before she can do so, however, Macbeth's hired ruffians arrive. They kill the boy and run after her to kill her off-stage.

Commentary
LINES 1-29
This is a scene of pathos which relieves the terror that has been so

predominant in this tragedy. Instead of participating in the nightmares of Macbeth, we witness the pitiful suffering and destruction of his innocent victims.

Lady Macduff's love for her children makes her upbraid her husband for his flight. We are to understand, however, that Macduff conceived it as his duty to his country to join Malcolm and seek the aid of England even though it might entail some risk to his family, whom he could not believe even Macbeth would slaughter. The owl, the bird of death, alluded to by Lady Macduff, should be associated with Macbeth because it shrieked all the night of the murder of Duncan. Thus it is not Macduff who is unnatural, but Macbeth.

LINES 30-63

The cleverness of Lady Macduff's son has the charm of childhood precociousness, a charm which may come off better on the stage than in reading, where it may seem rather artificial. Pathos and humor mingle, the mother's sadness and her commiseration for her defenseless son being balanced by the boy's delightful assurance in his wit. Dominating the dialogue is the audience's awareness that Macbeth has given orders that the castle be surprised and they killed. The boy's smart retort to his mother's calling him a poor bird, that traps are not set for such poor birds as he, and the joke about her marrying again are dramatically ironic in the light of this awareness.

LINES 64-84

In the presence of these murderers the pathetic, grieving woman and upbraiding wife becomes the great noblewoman proudly defiant in behalf of her lord. She, who had been implying that her husband is dead to her, tells the murderers that she hopes that her husband is "in no place so unsanctified" (80)—the words recall that Macduff is in the court of the "most pious" and "holy" Edward the Confessor (Act III, Sc. 6, 27, 30)— that such as they can reach him. Similarly, the boy, who had replied jestingly to Lady Macduff's statement that his father is a traitor—she meant that he had broken his marriage vow to protect her—replies indignantly to the same statement by the murderer. Affectionate to his mother, he is also high-spirited, and he dies bravely, calling upon his mother to run away after he himself has received his death-wound. As in the Banquo murder scene, where Banquo's dying words were that Fleance run away, the brutality of the muderers is contrasted with the tenderness and self-sacrifice of family love.

The murder of Lady Macduff and her son is the turning-point. It sets the seal on Macbeth as a tyrant and sets into motion the force that will destroy him. The angry and contemptuous words of the murderer to the son of Macduff—"egg," that is, unhatched chick, and "young fry" or spawn of treachery (82-83)—is significant in this connection. These are images of fertility. Macbeth, turned totally to destruction, is trying to strike at the future while it is yet in the seed, but nothing can prevent the future, the consequences of his own acts, from happening. In fact, he only hastens that future.

ACT IV • SCENE 3

Summary
In England Macduff urges Malcolm to lead an expedition against Macbeth. Malcolm, however, is suspicious of Macduff, as Macbeth had previously sent secret agents to him seeking to entice him to return to Scotland. He is convinced of Macduff's sincerity when, as a ruse to see Macduff's response, he falsely accuses himself of being so vice-ridden that he will be an even worse king than Macbeth. When Macduff turns away in passionate indignation and sorrow, Malcolm tells him the truth. Moreover, he informs him that an English army has already been gathered to invade Scotland on behalf of Malcolm. While Macduff is standing amazed at the good turn of events, Malcolm speaks to a doctor, who tells him that King Edward has been delayed because, with his miraculous power of curing the disease of scrofula by touching its victim, he has been detained by a horde of sufferers of the disease. Ross enters with fresh news of Scotland. He tells them that Scotland is in a worse plight than ever and, after some hesitation, tells Macduff of the slaughter of his wife and children. Macduff resolves to execute vengeance on the field of battle, and Malcolm expresses his certitude that they will triumph with the aid of heaven.

Commentary
LINES 1-139
This lengthy, discursive scene, sometimes regarded as too drawn out, furnishes a respite in the swift-moving action and presents a choric commentary on the evil of Macbeth, touching on a number of themes of the play.

Malcolm justifies his suspicion of Macduff by stating the difficulty of knowing where good is and where evil is when evil assumes the form of good. Yet despite the deceptiveness of evil in assuming the guise of good, good must maintain its own appearance. The difficulty in distinguishing between appearance and reality is increased by the fact that good may be corrupted into evil. Macbeth "was once thought honest" (13), just as the brightest of the angels, Lucifer, also fell (22).

Macbeth is thus identified with Lucifer, whose fall through ambition in seeking to supplant God set the pattern for evil human behavior. He is also spoken of as "black Macbeth" (52) and "devilish Macbeth" (117), and it is said of him that in the legions of hell there is not a "devil more damn'd/ In evils" (55-57) than he. Malcolm, on the other hand, is implicitly compared to Christ. He says that Macduff may think it politic to make a sacrificial offering of him, "a weak, poor, innocent lamb," in order to appease Macbeth, "an angry god" (16-17). The lamb is a symbol of Christ, and the angry god is one of the pagan gods who were thought to have become the devils of Christian theology.

When Malcolm speaks of his alleged vices, he reverses the actuality. He lists the kingly virtues to say that he does not have them, but it is in Macbeth that they are absent. His supposed disregard for "the sweet milk of concord" (98) recalls that Macbeth once had the "milk o' human kindness." But whereas Macbeth has brought disorder to Scotland, Malcolm, in reverse of his statement, will not. To test Macduff, Malcolm says that, compared with himself, Macbeth will seem to everyone to have been a lamb (54). Good, taking a cue from evil, has disguised itself to test good, just as evil, using deception, tempts those who may be prone to it.

LINES 139-159

The description of Edward the Confessor opposes the saintly king of England to the devilish king of Scotland. Edward's "heavenly gift of prophecy" (157) is a supernatural power derived from heaven in contrast with the power of the witches derived from hell. His miraculous cures contrast with the hurts which Macbeth inflicts upon Scotland. Again and again, Scotland has been personified and described as beaten down, driven, wounded, and bleeding (3-4, 31, 39-41). Macduff had asked when will Scotland see "wholesome days" (105) again. The answer is when it gains a king "full of grace" (159), as Edward is.

LINES 159-240

The theme of what constitutes a man is once more played upon when Macduff is informed of the murder of his wife and children. Malcolm urges him to struggle against his grief "like a man" (220); Macduff replies, "I shall do so;/ But I must also feel it as a man" (220-221). The gentler feelings of pity, love, and grief are as much a part of manhood as anger and courage. Macduff tempers his grief and contains his anger, resolving to seek revenge. This revenge, however, is a revenge on the field of battle by one whom the murder of his wife and children has made the symbol of outraged Scotland and an agent of divine justice.

Malcolm at the end of the scene states that God's angels are urging them on. His last line uses the recurring night-day antithesis, this time as a promise that Scotland is about to emerge out of the night which Macbeth has brought upon her.

ACT V • SCENE 1

Summary

Lady Macbeth's waiting gentlewoman recapitulates to a physician at the castle on Dunsinane Hill what she has witnessed. During this period, when Macbeth has been busy taking action against rebellion, she has seen Lady Macbeth walk in her sleep. As they are talking, Lady Macbeth enters sleepwalking. She speaks aloud, re-living the nights Duncan and Banquo were murdered and trying desperately to wipe imaginary blood off her hands. When she thinks that she has finally got them clean at last and raises them to her face to look at them more closely, she smells the odor of the blood and realizes that she can never rid herself of the remembrance of the crime. The physician and the gentlewoman look on in horror as Lady Macbeth betrays herself. When Lady Macbeth returns to bed, the physician comments that she needs a clergyman more than a doctor and orders the gentlewoman to remove from Lady Macbeth anything which she might use to inflict harm upon herself.

Commentary

The previous long scene gives the impression that a good deal of time has gone by since we last saw Lady Macbeth. Although, when she spoke to Macbeth at her last appearance, her nerve was strong, we have seen indications of the strain upon her. Her breakdown has therefore been prepared for.

The scene is in prose except for the doctor's concluding lines, which act as a choric commentary and bring the scene to an effective conclusion. Prose is the appropriate medium for the rest of the scene, as the regularity of meter would not befit Lady Macbeth's disjointed utterances. Moreover, the simple language of the gentlewoman, expressing the awed horror of ordinary persons in the face of a revealed monstrous evil, and the clinical, if similarly horrified, observations of the doctor are best couched in prose.

The presence of the doctor on the scene recalls the doctor in England who could not explain on the basis of scientific knowledge Edward's miraculous cures. So too this doctor states: "This disease is beyond my practice" (56). It is a matter of a sick soul rather than a sick body, and Lady Macbeth needs the divine rather than the physician (71). Matters concerned with the supernatural are in each instance beyond the ken of science. The supernatural, however, affects the natural.

The sleepwalking is highly dramatic in its revelation of that within Lady Macbeth which she had sought to suppress and also highly ironic. She had called upon night to come to hide her deed, but now she is afraid of the dark and has light by her when she goes to sleep. She had told Macbeth that a little water would clear them of the deed, but now in her sleep she continually washes her hands, seeking to get the blood off them. The shock which she received on going back to Duncan with the bloody daggers, a shock which she successfully suppressed, is revealed in her terrible question "Yet who would have thought the old man to have had so much blood in him?" (38-39).

Many of her sentences repeat or echo with ironic effect what she had said before. Compare 37-38 with Act I, Sc. 7, 78; or 43-44 with her contemptuous "O, these flaws and starts" (Act III, Sc. 4, 62) at the banquet scene. But at this very moment she is revealing her guilt, as she had rebuked Macbeth for doing. She repeats her command to Macbeth at the time of the Duncan murder to wash his hands, but she herself is now trying in vain to wash her own hands. Her "What's done cannot be undone" (64) echoes her previous "What's done is done" (Act III, Sc. 2, 12), but then she was saying to her husband that there is no point in thinking about the past, which cannot be changed. Now the words have the ring of despair: the horrible past cannot indeed be changed, nor can one escape from it. Finally, her concluding words remind us not only of Macduff's knocking at the gate when she told Macbeth that they must go to their bedroom to change their clothes; they remind us that Macbeth cannot sleep in his bed and that she cannot find true rest in sleep.

ACT V • SCENE 2

Summary

An army led by the Scotch nobles Menteith, Caithness, Angus, and Lennox is marching near Birnam Wood to join the English army led by Malcolm, Siward, an old English general, and Macduff. The news is that Macbeth is fortifying Dunsinane Castle in a mad frenzy. Many are coming over to the rebels, and those who serve under Macbeth do so unwillingly.

Commentary

This is the first of a number of short scenes in this act, which alternates between the opposition and Macbeth. On the modern stage, where the curtain goes down after each scene so that scenery may be changed, such short scenes offer problems and may cause the action to lag. The Elizabethan stage, however, had no elaborate scenery and no curtain. Each scene followed immediately after the preceding one, making possible swift-moving action and emphasizing the contrast between scenes. We alternate between Macbeth's frenzied defiance and the opposition's confident patriotism.

The Scottish nobles continue the imagery of disease to indicate the life-giving qualities of the opposition to Macbeth. The wrongs against Malcolm and Macduff would stir a paralytic to action (3-5). Macbeth is said to be "mad" (13) and "cannot buckle his distemper'd cause/ Within the belt of rule" (15-16). Here we have a figure that is at once a disease image ("distemper'd" means swollen with dropsy), a clothing image, and a disorder image. A succeeding clothing image (20-22) suggests a picture not of a bloated Macbeth but of a dwindling Macbeth, evil falling away in the presence of advancing good. His "pester'd" (23) or tormented mind behaves erratically. Malcolm is the "med'cine" (27) of the sick country. His men are ready to shed their last drop of blood as a "purge" (28) for Scotland's illness. Blood here is life-giving, unlike the blood which Angus speaks of as "sticking" on Macbeth's hands (16).

This revolt, though good, must, it is stated, remind Macbeth of his own breach of faith (18). The invasion from without and the aid it receives from within are also reminiscent of the Norwegian invasion aided by the Thane of Cawdor which Macbeth had put down at the beginning of the play. Here, however, the reigning monarch is an absolute tyrant and the one opposing him is the rightful heir to the throne. Moreover, the joining together of the English and Scottish forces foreshadows the later organic union of the United Kingdom and is therefore proper.

ACT V • SCENE 3

Summary

Macbeth at Dunsinane is in a frenzy about the defection of his thanes, but he holds to the belief that no rebellion against him can succeed until Birnam Wood comes to Dunsinane. He rages when he hears about the English force and orders his armor to be put on so that he may be in readiness for battle. The doctor tells him that Lady Macbeth is not physically ill but deeply troubled mentally. When he tells Macbeth that for such mental illness there is nothing he can so, Macbeth replies furiously. Speaking impatiently to his squire, talking first about his wife's illness and then about the illness of Scotland, he is distracted.

Commentary

In the preceding scene reference to Birnam Wood and Dunsinane reminded us of the apparition's prediction, to which we see Macbeth now clinging in desperation. Also, the description of Macbeth has prepared us for his outburst at the frightened servant and his impatience with his squire. He commands him to put his armor on him even though it is not yet time for battle and the armor will tire him, is fretful when the squire is not as fast as he wishes, and leaves before a piece of armor has been put on.

In the midst of his frenzy he betrays a weariness with life. When he asks the doctor whether he cannot erase thoughts deeply imprinted in the brain or relieve the oppressed heart by some drug that will confer the sweetness of utter forgetfulness (43), he reveals his own tormented conscience and his longing for peace, the peace which he had given Duncan. In another speech he says, "I have liv'd long enough: my way of life/ Is fall'n into the sere, the yellow leaf" (22-23). Actually, an analysis of the time scheme shows that there has been no lapse of years, but Shakespeare, in what has been called "double time," often gives an impression of the passage of time at variance with the reality. Here the impression is that Macbeth has endured a lifetime of suffering. Moreover, in his old age he cannot expect that which should accompany old age—there is an implicit contrast here with the old age of Duncan—such as honor, love, obedience, friends. In his loneliness he is aware of the precious human values he has given up, and this awareness helps to maintain some sympathy for him. Yet, lonely though he be, he continues to fight with the courage of despair, a courage that echoes and yet contrasts with his courage at the beginning of the play.

The soul weariness and the frenzy of Macbeth are expressed in continued disease imagery. Although he holds himself to be immune from the sickness of fear, he does admit for a moment that he is "sick at heart" when he perceives his isolation. Nevertheless a little later he states that success in the battle will "cheer me ever" (21). He is still deceiving himself, thinking as always that one more thing will make him happy. He is equally blind when he speaks of the disease of Scotland (50-56), not realizing that he is the source of it.

ACT V • SCENE 4

Summary
Malcolm orders his troops to hack off the boughs of Birnam Wood to bear in front of them, thus obscuring the number of men from Macbeth's scouts. The news that Malcolm and his generals have received is that Macbeth, seeing that he is losing men to the enemy and doubtful of those remaining, has resolved not to give battle but to withstand a siege in well-fortified and well-provisioned Dunsinane.

Commentary
We see now how Birnam Wood will come to Dunsinane and wait to see how Macbeth will be killed although this cannot be done by a man born of woman. The solving of the riddles helps to maintain interest as the inevitable conclusion approaches.

ACT V • SCENE 5

Summary
Macbeth proclaims that he will wait out the invading forces, who must succumb to the famine and pestilence that attends a siege. Just then, a cry of women is heard. On inquiry he learns that Lady Macbeth is dead. He responds without grief, soliloquizing on the meaninglessness of life. The future is without any significance. It is not anything to be striven for or prevented, for nothing in life is worth fighting for. Lady Macbeth would have died sometime in the future if she had not died now, and it makes no difference just when, for each "tomorrow" is a step, no different from the one before or after on the monotonous course toward the grave. When a messenger comes in to say that he has seen Birnam Wood moving, Macbeth, on finding the seemingly impossible prediction coming true, orders his men out: at least, they will die fighting.

Commentary
The cry of the women, which once would have caused the chill of terror, now does not even startle Macbeth. He has become inured to terror, a man at last, according to the criterion of manliness he has accepted. The irony is that in having become such a man he has become drained of all feeling so that he receives the death of his wife, who had taught him this concept of manliness, with the indifference of apathy. He has become alienated, has come to feel that life is meaningless and futile.

In Macbeth's famous soliloquy, once more life is compared to a drama on the stage, this time, however, to convey the sense of its brevity, transcience, and illusoriness. In saying "Life's but a walking shadow" (24), Macbeth is echoing the Bible, but not to contrast the insubstantiality of life on earth with the glory of God or the life hereafter: for him life ends in "dusty death" (23). "Shadow" suggests "actor," for actors were often spoken of as shadows, mere imitations of life. Life is a "poor player," for the actor, no matter with what violence of passion he conducts himself, finds his little time on the stage soon over and he himself only a rapidly disappearing memory. Just so with life itself; the real thing is just as transitory as the imitation. Even more horrible and pathetic, it is not even a coherent work of art; it is rather like the wild, confused babbling of an idiot, a story without a meaning. This is what Macbeth has finally come to feel: behind the appearance of order in life is the ultimate reality—nothingness. All of his passionate strivings have been for naught.

This is a powerful and disturbing view of life, but we see it as the consequence of Macbeth's having severed himself from mankind. As it is being expressed, we see the forces of order on the march. The Scottish nobles would gladly give up their lives for their cause. It is the sense of being engaged in a collective human enterprise that makes life have meaning.

Macbeth, however, though weary of life, intends to go on fighting. He is ready to destroy the entire universe with himself. This extraordinary egotism is all that he has left. Aghast by the messenger's news that Birnam Wood seems to be moving towards Dunsinane, he nevertheless orders his men to leave the castle to engage in hand-to-hand combat. Disregarding his own previous words that he can withstand a siege, he thus ironically causes the prophecies to come true. Proceeding in desperation, he as always brings his destruction upon himself.

ACT V • SCENE 6

Summary
On a plain before the castle, Malcolm commands his men to lay down their boughs, for they have come close enough. He marshalls the order of battle.

Commentary
Good has hidden itself, but now it shows itself as it is. Malcolm's command to his army that it proceed "according to our order" (6) contrasts Malcolm as the representative of order with Macbeth as the representative of disorder.

ACT V • SCENE 7

Summary
Macbeth, fighting desperately, confronts Young Siward, the son of the English general, and kills him. Macbeth takes this as assurance that no man born of woman can harm him. As he leaves the stage, Macduff enters, looking for him, and hearing a great noise off-stage, indicating that a great warrior is fighting there, follows it. Malcolm and old Siward enter, and we learn that the castle has been given up by Macbeth's men, who are really on the side of Malcolm.

Commentary

Macbeth seems to know that he must die and fights with the desperation of a wounded animal, comparing himself to a bear beset by dogs in the Elizabethan sport of bear-baiting. Yet even now, after so many deceptions by the powers of evil, he clings to the prophecy that he cannot be hurt by a man born of woman. His slaying of Young Siward, who has met him undaunted, even though he regards Macbeth as a diabolical figure, encourages him to continue. At this final moment he seems invincible.

Macduff, in proclaiming that he will fight with none but Macbeth, reminds us that as the symbol of outraged Scotland he is the person destined to kill Macbeth. His reference to the "wretched Kernes" (17), Irish freebooters and irregulars, with whom he will not fight, recalls the "merciless Macdonwald" (Act I, Sc. 2, 9), who also employed these mercenaries. Disorder has repeated itself and will again be quelled.

ACT V • SCENE 8

Summary

Macduff, coming upon Macbeth, tells him to turn and fight. Macbeth does not wish to do so, saying that he has too much of Macduff's blood upon him already, and tells Macduff that it is no use for Macduff to try to kill him, as no man born of woman can hurt him. When Macduff replies that Macbeth should despair of his charm protecting him, for Macduff was "from his mother's womb/ Untimely ripp'd," Macbeth is for a moment daunted and refuses to fight. On being told, however, that he will be made captive to be exhibited to the populace as a monster, he determines to fight to the end and is slain.

Commentary

Macbeth rejects the idea of imitating the ancient Romans, who thought it a point of honor to commit suicide when faced with overwhelming odds, thus triumphing in a sense over their opponents. With animal ferocity, he wishes to kill as long as he sees opposing soldiers. The epithet "Hell-hound" (3) which Macduff uses in addressing him combines an animal image with a diabolical image.

Macduff's announcement of how he came into the world is portentous. It is as if, a bloody prodigy of Nature, he was prematurely called into being to meet the harsh needs of the time. He is the bloody child, once pitiably weak, who is now terrifyingly invincible.

Macbeth's reluctance to fight Macduff is caused in good part by the prophecy "Beware Macduff." Nevertheless, his statement that there is too much of Macduff's blood on him already must be accepted, for it is in keeping with his expressed wish to the doctor that certain memories could be extirpated from the brain. Here, as in his expression of his desolation in his later years, we see that, despite the epithets directed at him, he has not quite lost all his humanity. Terrible in his isolation, he does not leave the stage without the audience's feeling some sense of loss for the extinguished

57

glory of this figure of darkness. His fear of Macduff, the fear of a moment, is caused by a sense of helplessness at having been deserted by fate. However, he summons up his resolution and dies with satanic defiance.

CLOSING SCENE

Summary

In the castle Malcolm expresses concern at the absence of Macduff and Young Siward. Ross informs Siward that his son died on the field of battle. Siward, on learning that his son died bravely, says that he could not have died better and gives him up to God. Macduff enters with Macbeth's head mounted on a pole and hails Malcolm as king of Scotland, a cry taken up by all. Malcolm rewards his friends by making them earls, the first of that title in Scotland, and, promising to do everything necessary to set the kingdom to rights, invites every one to witness his coronation at Scone. Lady Macbeth, he announces parenthetically, died, apparently by suicide.

Commentary

Some editors print this scene as a continuation of the previous scene rather than a new one, with a gathering on the field of battle to the flourish of trumpets. Others, however, print it as a separate scene, with Malcolm remaining in the castle.

Siward's son, we were told earlier (Act V, Sc. 3, 9-11), was one of many young men who proclaimed that he had come to manhood by joining the army. These young men are representative of the future which Macbeth had sought to suppress. Their rising up against Macbeth, like the rising of Birnam Wood, is indicative of Nature itself, violated by Macbeth, moving to expel him. Young Siward only lived until he proved himself to be a man in battle and then "like a man he died." It was not only, however, his personal courage that established his manhood but his acting as "God's soldier" in doing his patriotic duty.

Malcolm, surrounded by his "kingdom's pearl", occupies the proper place of a king, the center of things. His proclamation of his thanes as earls suggests the beginning of a new epoch in which there is a greater social stability with a more sharply defined social hierarchy. It recalls Duncan's promise that when Malcolm will be invested with his title "signs of nobleness, like stars, shall shine/ On all deservers" (Act I, Sc. 4, 40-41). Malcolm uses the same imagery of nature's bounty as did Duncan. His promise that whatever is necessary to be done will be done "in measure, time, and place" is a promise of the restoration of order.

Character Sketches
Macbeth

COURAGEOUS, STRONG, A GOOD GENERAL
1. Co-leader with Banquo of Duncan's army.

2. Spoken of more frequently than Banquo and therefore must be considered the senior.

3. First engagement of the battle is represented as having been won by his personal powers and generalship. See Act I, Sc. 2, 14. "But all's too weak ... Till he faced the slave."

4. Undismayed when faced by a new threat from the army of the rebel reinforced "with terrible numbers" by the King of Norway, "assisted by the most disloyal traitor, the Thane of Cawdor." Victorious again "Bellona's bridegroom."

5. As he becomes degraded he loses some fearlessness, Act IV, Sc. 1, 84, "That I may tell pale-hearted fear it lies"; but whenever the prospect of action appears his courage never fails him.

6. Lady Macbeth gets him to act by appealing to his manhood and courage, Act I, Sc. 7, 49, "When you durst do it ... more the man."

7. The old courage and strength show themselves in his fight with young Siward and in the early part of his fight with Macduff.

A MORAL COWARD
1. Brave when it comes to action but when he starts thinking he hesitates and fears and has to be goaded into action by his wife or by the sense of security which he obtains from his contact with the witches.

2. Changed his mind six times before murdering Duncan: (a) Had made up his mind to it before meeting the witches. (b) Their prophecy that he would be king makes him decide to leave it to fate. (c) Duncan's announcement that Malcolm is to be his successor presents a difficulty which he must "oe'rleap." (d) Suffers a change of heart before he reaches home until (e) his wife persuades him that it can be done safely. (f) Leaves the banquet and decides not to do it. (g) Is goaded by Lady Macbeth to make up his mind finally to do the murder.

3. Fears Banquo because he recognizes in him a moral courage which Macbeth lacked—Banquo kept his "bosom franchised and allegiance clear."

4. Hated and feared Macduff, too, because he felt his own "genius rebuked" by Macduff's moral superiority. "Thou shalt not live That I may tell pale-hearted fear it lies ..."

5. Does not show a single example of moral uprightness in the play.

6. Does not fear the moral consequences of his sin. "We'd jump the life to come," Act. I, Sc. 7, 7.

7. His whole story after the death of Duncan is one of continuous moral degradation. He is in a savage frenzy when he plans the murder of Macduff's family. His cruelty is so great that "Sighs and groans and shrieks that rend the air are made, not mark'd."

8 So far does he sink in moral degradation that even his enemies say half-pityingly:
   "Who then shall blame
   His pester'd senses to recoil and start,
   When all that is within him does condemn
   Itself for being there?"

AMBITIOUS

1. There can be no doubt that Macbeth had entertained the possibility of being king some day. His success in battle would serve to intensify his ambition.

2. More than that, it seems clear that the thought of murder had already occurred to him, Act I, Sc. 3, 57, "great prediction/Of noble having ... That he seems rapt withal ..." and Act I, Sc. 7, 48-53, "What beast was't, then,/That made you break this enterprise to me?" Act I, Sc. 3, 140, "My thought, whose murder yet is but fantastical."

3. When Macbeth "starts at the fair-sounding" predictions of the witches (Act I, Sc. 3) it is because they have startled him by putting his thoughts into actual words.

4. His "rapt" behavior, his wish "Would they had stayed," and his brooding over the prophecy all seem to indicate a more than casual concern.

5. The witches' prophecies encouraged this ambition to be king.

6. He himself confesses "vaulting ambition" (Act I, Sc. 7) that will carry him to murder now that Duncan has circumvented fate (Act I, Sc. 3, 144) "If chance ... may crown me" by naming Malcolm successor to the throne.

7. Lady Macbeth's speech (Act I, Sc. 5) sums up his character early in the play. It reveals that Macbeth was a very ordinary man whose ambition was great and who wished to stand well with the world. But he was unprincipled and refrained from wrong-doing only from custom or from fear of being found out. It is his unprincipled ambition and his crimes to attain that ambition that make the theme of this great tragedy.

SUPERSTITIOUS AND IMAGINATIVE

1. Macbeth's power and his successes made him conjure up alluring thoughts of kingship.

2. His fluctuating will make him subject to the over-mastering character of his wife in the early part of the play.

3. His imagination, controlled neither by moral considerations nor by education made him a ready victim to the tempting voices of superstition.

4. Before the murder we find his "function/Is smother'd in surmise" (Act I, Sc. 3, 141) when he allows his imagination to roam uncontrolled. Moreover so active and powerful is his imagination that it always creates "present fears" which "are less than horrible imaginings" (Act I, Sc. 3, 139).

5. His superstition is shown by his susceptibility to the influence of the witches—more marked by contrast with Banquo's cautious indifference.

6. It is also seen in the "air-drawn dagger" and in the hysteria of fear which seizes him after the murder of Duncan.

7. But, most important of all, he sees the ghost of Banquo at the banquet. The mental excitement created made him reveal much that he would have liked to remain unknown, and in this way hastened his ruin and punishment.

8. It was his superstition that made him accept so unquestioningly the promises of the apparitions.

9. And when circumstances became difficult it was his superstition that made him cling to these promises until events proved how equivocal and misleading they were.

10. When he is in throes of his imaginative hallucinations, abstract ideas appear before him in concrete form. The imagery of his speeches becomes intense, condensed and highly figurative. We find this particularly in the scenes surrounding the murder of Duncan. The more intense his excitement, the more vivid and intense does his language become to mirror the emotional strain of the scene.

LOVED HIS WIFE

1. Shared his joys with her—sent her a letter describing the witches' prophecies—was going to wait until Banquo was out of the way before disclosing this fact to her.

2. Accepts her guidance and advice and consults her concerning his plans.

3. Is affectionate in his action toward her and uses terms of endearment when speaking to her—"my dearest love" (Act I, Sc. 5, 58).

4. Keeps to himself when planning the murder of Banquo and Fleance so that she will not have to share the strain.

HIS CHARACTER DETERIORATED

1. Once she has launched him on his career of crime Lady Macbeth loses her control over him.

2. Once the savior of his country, a "valiant cousin!" a "worthy gentleman," he follows his murder of Duncan with the quick murder of the two sleepy grooms.

3. He does not need to be urged to the deed in planning the murder of Banquo and of Fleance.

4. His degradation carries him to the level where he vents his savage frenzy upon the innocent heads of "His [Macduff's] wife, his babes ..."

5. Scotland suffers from his boundless cruelty: "Sighs and groans and shrieks that rend the air, are made, not mark'd."

6. He becomes distrustful, "There's not a one of them but in his house I keep a servant fee'd."

7. He becomes cruel and treacherous; the voice of conscience within him is gone; he no longer hesitates to follow courses of evil: "The very firstlings of my heart shall be The firstlings of my hand."

8. But the tragedy is still tragedy because he reveals to us that he is suffering a living hell in the midst of fears, amongst those that hate him but dare not show it, without the blessing of sleep "that knits up the ravell'd sleave of care," in a life that can know no rest. His punishment is as great as his crimes.

Lady Macbeth

1. Not a monster lacking in humanity but possessed feelings and tenderness natural to a woman. Her motives and other influences caused her to suppress natural instincts and to assist in planning and execution of a murder.

2. Possessed majesty and courtliness suited to a great queen—spoiled by the evil of her ambitions.

LOVED AND ADMIRED HER HUSBAND

1. As she reads his letter to her, her comments show that she knows her husband's character, admires his greatness and intends to help him achieve his ambition.

2. Knows his weaknesses and going to use her own strong will to keep him from weakening on the course he has planned for himself. "Hie thee hither, That I may pour my spirits in thine ear ... crown'd withal" (Act I, Sc. 5).

3. Their first meeting is affectionate, "Great Glamis," "My dearest love." Throughout the play their love shown in "gentle my lord," and "worthy thane" and "dear wife," "my love" and "dearest chuck."

4. After the murder of Duncan she selflessly forces all her strength to give Macbeth courage and to support him in his weakness.

5. After the banquet scene when he has betrayed them she tries to comfort him, "You lack the season of all natures, sleep" (Act III, Sc. 4, 142).

HAD FEMININE QUALITIES

1. Devoted to her husband.

2. A gracious hostess and a regal queen.

3. A mother. She has given suck and knows "how tender 'tis to love the babe" that milks her.

4. Her cruelty is not natural but results from her superhuman will through which she is able to repress her true nature, "Come, you spirits ... unsex me here, And fill me ... direst cruelty" (Act I, Sc. 5, 41).

5. Is able to steel herself to the point where she is going to commit the crime to spare her husband that necessity, but is prevented by an unforseen feeling of tenderness against which she had not thought to steel herself. "Had he not resembled My father as he slept, I had done't" (Act II, Sc. 2, 12).

6. Her motive for the crime was her unselfish love for Macbeth, for whom she would like to get the throne so that he might achieve his highest ambition.

7. If one accepts the genuineness of her fainting spell one can ascribe it to the further manifestation of her feminine qualities.

HAS STRENGTH OF WILL AND SINGLENESS OF PURPOSE

1. Is called upon several times to exert her great strength of will to force Macbeth to the point of action (see note on Macbeth's character, point 2 under heading "A Moral Coward").

2. Only strength of will could have forced her to return to the chamber of death to place the daggers beside the sleeping grooms.

3. In contrast with Macbeth she is not bothered by imagination, hence her singleness of purpose. She sees no ghosts or witches; she sees only the direct road of action toward success.

4. She drives from her mind and her thoughts all feelings of compunction. "The attempt and not the deed confound us," she says, and, "What need we fear who knows it, when none can call our power to account." Beyond the successful attainment of her husband's goal she refuses to allow herself to see. Macbeth's strength lies in action, hers in the power of her mind.

5. Exhibits great presence of mind and quick perception in the banquet scene. She is not able to prevent Macbeth from revealing his guilt, but in her actions she salvages as much as possible. At his first outbreak she explains that it is a long-standing illness that is responsible for his behavior, and with the second outbreak she breaks up the banquet in as orderly a fashion as it was possible to do.

HER WEAKENING

1. Once we have established that she behaved in an unnatural way we recognize that she must have been under terrific strain.

2. Through force of will she stifled her conscience. She did not allow herself the relief of outward expression of remorse.

3. Her fainting spell may have been her first evidence of weakness, caused by her realization that Macbeth had gotten beyond her control and had committed them both to a continuing career of guilt and crime.

4. Shakespeare prepared us throughout the play for her eventual breakdown. Perhaps it is premonition of her own fate that makes her say to her husband, "These deeds must not be thought/After these ways; so, it will make us mad," (Act II, Sc. 2, 32).

5. When, as in the sleep-walking scene, her mind at last gives way under continued strain she reveals the true nature which she had tried to repress. Her agitated sleep, her three heart-rending "Oh's" reveal a heart "sorely charged."

6. Her natural abhorrence of blood, which she had stifled in order to encourage her husband, now reveals itself pathetically, "Here's the smell of the blood still; All the perfumes of Arabia will not sweeten this little hand. Oh, oh, oh!" (Act V, Sc. 1, 59).

7. At sight of such suffering we cannot help but be sympathetic. We agree with the doctor: "More needs she the divine than the physician" (Act V, Sc. 1, 74).

8. We are warned of her death, too, when the doctor tells the gentlewoman to "Remove from her the means of all annoyance."

9. Her death is sudden (the shrieks of woman) and self-inflicted. "'Tis thought, by self and violent hands Took off her life." Only in death could she find relief and rest.

King Duncan

Born out of his proper age into a century of intrigue and violence and offering a mark to rebels, traitors and ambitious aspirants to the throne. He is of too refined and peaceful a nature to cope with those who would contend with him.

WEAK
1. At the beginning of the play he shows up the superior qualities of Macbeth by contrast with his own incompetence.

2. He commits into Macbeth's hands the leading of his armies—a position which he should himself have undertaken.

3. Shows an emotional weakness in his over-gratitude to Macbeth and to Banquo. "My plenteous joys ... in drops of sorrow" (Act. I, Sc. 4).

4. Shows that he is a poor judge of human nature. "There's no art To find the mind's construction in the face ... An absolute trust" (Act I, Sc. 4).

5. Also shows his poor judgment in his too great trustfulness. Lavishes favors on his "peerless kinsman." Visits Macbeth's castle and places himself too freely into his hands.

6. Shows poor judgment in choosing the time to announce that Malcolm was heir to the crown.

After his death—and even before it, new light is shed on Duncan's character. Now he serves a different purpose in being contrasted with Macbeth. This time he is portrayed as "the gracious Duncan" to accentuate Macbeth's villainy in committing murder. Macbeth enumerates his virtues before the murder.

Banquo

Acts as a foil, or contrast, to Macbeth. Both are brave and successful generals; both are exposed to the same temptations, but because of the difference of characters their careers and actions present a strong contrast.

There are two interpretations of Banquo's character. The one absolves him of all guilt but accuses him of an irresolution that brought about his death. The other considers him a passive accomplice to Macbeth's crimes and blames his inaction and lack of suspicion upon his belief of the witches' prophecy connecting Banquo's descendants with the throne of Scotland.

Both will be presented here although most opinions favor the first mentioned above. We must remember that Shakespeare would do nothing to antagonize King James I who is supposed to have been in lineal descent from Banquo.

BRAVE
1. No less brave than Macbeth. Both are mentioned together "As cannons overcharged with double cracks" (Act I, Sc. 2, 36).

2. Macbeth says of him:

   " 'tis much he dares,
      And, to that dauntless temper of his mind. . . . (Act III, Sc. 1, 50)

3. At the same time he is not foolhardy but,

   "He hath a wisdom [prudence] that doth guide his valour
      To act in safety" (Act III, Sc. 1, 50)

MODEST AND UNENVIOUS
1. Duncan praises him:

                    "Noble Banquo
      That hath no less deserved, nor must be known
      No less to have done so; let me infold thee
      And hold thee to my heart;"
   Banquo modestly replies:
                    "There if I grow,
      The harvest is your own;" (Act I, Sc. 4)

2. Banquo has evidently been praising Macbeth to Duncan in the silent dramatic by-play which must go on while Macbeth speaks his soliloquy, because Duncan's speech immediately afterward indicates this (Act I, Sc. 4).

HONEST AND REFINED

1. His speech before Macbeth's castle (Act I, Sc. 6) and his imagery while talking to Fleance (Act II, Sc. 1) are evidence of a refined and poetic nature.

2. His honesty is shown in his struggles against temptation and the evil thoughts that beset him. Only in sleep does his power of resistance weaken.

   > "A heavy summons . . . that nature/Gives way to in repose" (Act II, Sc. 1)

CARELESS AND IRRESOLUTE

These two weaknesses in his nature brought him to his death.

1. He suspects Macbeth: "I fear Thou play'dst most foully for't" (Act III, Sc. 1, 2-3), yet he does nothing in self-defense.

2. He seems deliberately to shut his eyes to Macbeth's crime against Duncan. He seems, too, to have gone so far in believing the prophecies as to consider the murder inevitable. This passiveness is not without guilt since he, too, is going to gain:
   > "it was said
   > It should not stand in thy posterity,
   > But that myself should be the root and father
   > Of many kings." (Act III, Sc. 1, 3)

CONTRAST WITH MACBETH

1. (a) Witches represent evil ambitions of Macbeth. (b) Their prophecy concerning Banquo shows that his ambition was not as pressing brutal, or selfish as Macbeth's.

2. (a) Macbeth becomes excited at the witches' prophecies and is inclined to believe them. (b) Banquo considers them "instruments of darkness" which "Win us with honest trifles, to betray's/In deepest consequence" (Act I, Sc. 3, 126).

3. Both are superstitious, Banquo with some reservations.

4. Both are ambitious. (i)(a) Macbeth's ambition leads him to a career of crime. (b) Banquo goes so far as to pray "the merciful heavens" to help him control his ambition. (ii)(a) Macbeth's ambition is for himself first. Later he tries to have both Banquo and Fleance murdered so that the throne would continue in Macbeth's line and not in Banquo's. (b) Banquo is content that his descendants should be kings. As far as he himself is concerned he wishes to keep his "bosom franchised and allegiance clear."

5. (a) Macbeth fears and distrusts Banquo:"Our fears in Banquo/Stick deep . . .There is none but he / Whose being I do fear" (Act III, Sc.1). (b) Banquo does not fear Macbeth. He does, however, suspect him of murdering Duncan. His lack of caution makes possible his death at the hands of Macbeth's murderers.

6. (a) Macbeth is constantly plotting. (b) Banquo is open and honest in nature. He is much more naive than Macbeth .

These points are mentioned by those who consider Banquo guilty:

1. He knows the witches' prophecies about Macbeth.

2. He saw Macbeth start and realized the guilt in Macbeth's mind.

3. He covers up for Macbeth who is distracted by the witches' prophecies.

4. He tries twice to engage Macbeth in talk about the prophecies and is put off both times by Macbeth.

5. **Although he worries about the witches he is not suspicious enough** when he encounters Macbeth late at night near Duncan's chamber and carrying a dagger. If he were suspicious he should not have left the scene.

6. His behavior upon the discovery of the murder is not sufficiently surprised or horrified. This would indicate that he was prepared for such an event.

Macduff

Plays a very small part in the early portion of the play. With the murder of Banquo, however, he comes into prominence and is important in the shaping of the course of events.

NOBLE, WISE AND CLEAR-SIGHTED
1. Macbeth feels himself "rebuked" before Macduff's moral superiority and hates and fears him for it.

2. On the morning of the murder it was to have been his duty to awaken the king—a position of some trust and importance.

3. When he hears that Macbeth slew Duncan's chamberlains Macduff sternly rebukes him with "Wherefore did you so?"

4. Seems to have been suspicious of Macbeth from the very first— didn't attend coronation at Scone and expressed his fears concerning Macbeth in "Lest our old robes sit easier than our new."

CONTRAST TO BANQUO

1. Banquo kept his suspicions to himself. Macduff uses "broad words" (Act III, Sc. 6, 21) and succeeds in winning the active hostility of Macbeth.

2. He did not attend coronation, Banquo did.

3. Nor did he intend to be present at Macbeth's banquet and Banquo would have been there if he could. It was his absence at the banquet that made Macbeth turn his anger directly upon Macduff.

4. Banquo passively disloyal to Duncan, Macduff intensely loyal to Duncan and Duncan's true heirs.

5. Flees to England in order to offer aid to Malcolm.

LOYAL AND PATRIOTIC

1. Offers his assistance to Malcolm the true heir.

2. Puts country above home and family when he flees to England and leaves his castle at the mercy of the tyrannous usurper.

3. Convinces the cautious Malcolm of his loyalty by the sincerity of his grief when he feels he can no longer condone Malcolm's confession of faults.

4. When Ross enters the scene to join Malcolm and Macduff, the latter questions him first concerning Scotland and then asks about his family's welfare.

A MAN OF ACTION AND OF FEW WORDS

Macbeth too was a man of action but frequently he handicapped himself in action by being swept away in his own storm of words.

1. Macduff is silent while other leaders discuss plans or prospects (Act V, Sc. 4) or speaks only to urge "industrious soldiership."

2. When he meets Macbeth face to face on the battlefield he wastes no time in breath-taking talk: "I have no words: My voice is in my sword" (Act V, Sc. 3, 6)

3. He deliberately failed to tell his wife of his flight to England so that she might not be molested by those who sought to learn his whereabouts. For his mistake and his over-zealousness he paid a terrible price. He became directly involved and thus serves his purpose as *the instrument of fate—Macbeth's nemesis.*

Malcolm

1. At the beginning of the play he is yet a young boy, too young to participate in battle.

2. He is named heir by his father in presence of the leading nobles.

3. Upon the discovery of the murder he is wise enough to realize that he is not safe and, along with Donalbain, he decides to escape to safety.

4. When we next see him he is a grown man.

5. He is highly enough thought of to be assisted by the English king with an army to be under his leadership.

6. He has learned to be cautious. Macbeth has evidently tried several times to trick him into returning and so Macduff is naturally suspected.

7. Once he is convinced of Macduff's sincerity he is decisive in putting himself at Macduff's disposal.

8. He abjures his false self-accusations of bad character and reveals himself a worthy son of a "most sainted king" and saintly mother, and the worthy nephew of a saintly uncle, King Edward the Confessor.

9. As the campaign progresses his character seems to develop and his acceptance of the throne is done in truly regal manner.

Ross

1. News carrier of the play.

2. Reports result of battle to Duncan.

3. Tells Macbeth of his new title Thane of Cawdor.

4. Tells Macduff of the death of his wife and children.

5. Announces death of young Siward to his father.

6. Remains loyal to Macbeth up to the banquet scene.

7. Appears to be of a gentle kindly nature.

Lennox

1. Takes practically no part in the action.

2. Remains with Macbeth until banquet scene.

3. Crosses to English side to join Malcolm's invading army.

4. Keen observer: "his grooms, *as it seemed,* had done it."

5. His ironic comments suggest more than they say and are master-pieces of sarcasm, especially in Act III, Sc. 6, 1-24.

Points of Interest

Shakespeare has made use of many dramatic devices to heighten the interest in the play. The following are some of the most important:

Suspense Occurs

1. When we await Macbeth's final decision to murder Duncan.

2. When Macbeth waits outside Duncan's door for the signal to enter and commit the murder.

3. When we wonder if the Macbeths are going to be discovered.

4. In waiting for Macduff to return from the murder chamber.

5. To a lesser extent before the murder of Banquo.

6. And in the latter part of the play while we wait to see the way the prophecies of the apparitions are going to work out.

Dramatic Irony

When the words or actions of a character have a significance opposite to that which is generally understood and that double meaning is perceived by the audience and only one meaning by the character concerned, the double significance is called dramatic irony. Examples in *Macbeth* are:

1. Duncan's remark, "There's no art to find the mind's construction in the face" is followed by the immediate entry of Macbeth. Duncan's second, and fatal, mistake in character reading is ironical.

2. Duncan, entering the castle where the audience has seen and heard his murder planned, talks of the beauty of the castle.

3. Banquo's promise to be present at the banquet (Act III).

4. Banquo's appearance as a ghost each time Macbeth mentions his absence and expresses a wish that he were there.

5. The revelations of the apparitions and their seeming promise of

immunity and impunity for Macbeth are ironical in their double sense.

The Oracular or Prophetic Element
IN THE FIRST HALF OF THE PLAY
1. The three prophecies of the witches concerning Macbeth.

2. Their prophecy concerning Banquo's descendants.

3. When the first two come true for Macbeth he commits murder to bring the third about.

4. He commits murder to try to forestall the prophecy that promised Banquo's descendants the Scottish throne, but he failed in his efforts to frustrate the prophecy. All of the prophecies come true.

IN THE SECOND HALF OF THE PLAY
1. Here again there are three predictions that affect Macbeth. This time they are calculated to bring about his ruin. They sound fair and promising but only because he wants to believe them. Unfortunately for him, they were capable of double interpretation, and brought about his ruin.

2. The Banquo prediction in the second half is a reiteration of that contained in the first half, namely, the show of eight kings. Here again Macbeth is powerless to prevent the fulfillment of fate's promise to Banquo.

Nemesis
The Emperor in the "Mikado" defined nemesis when he determined to make the punishment suit the crime. Nemesis is just or retributive punishment. The play *Macbeth* is full of the working of nemesis.

1. Macbeth's ambition leads him to believe the prophecies of the Weird Sisters; it is this belief that brings about his downfall.

2. He murders Duncan and Macduff kills him.

3. Banquo fails to act in protection of himself and of others, and his inaction is responsible for his own death.

4. Duncan is a weak king and falls victim to the ambitions of a strong man.

5. Lady Macbeth has to force Macbeth to commit the murder and has to stand by helplessly while he continues on his unbridled career of murder.

6. The second part of her punishment is the torture of personal remorse which will not let her rest and leads her to madness and to suicide.

7. Macduff makes the mistake of overzealous haste and rashness. He leaves his loved ones unprotected and suffers the terrible punishment of losing them all.

8. Malcolm's well-rounded character—his strength of mind and his upright morality are rewarded with victory and the throne.

The Spectacular
Provided by four scenes:

1. The Witches.

2. The Banquet Scene.

3. The Sleep-Walking Scene.

4. The Battle at the end.

Spectacular, defined as the element of spectacle, is also present in *Macbeth*. Court scenes, banquet scenes and battle scenes are all potentially picturesque. In actual production of the play costumes add a colorful touch and stage settings are calculated to please the eye as well.

The Supernatural
The interest of the supernatural lies in the unusual, the unseen, the unknown. It has no less appeal to us than it had to the audience of Shakespeare's own day, albeit we lack their belief in witchcraft.

The supernatural occurs:

1. In all the appearances of the witches.

2. In the strange behavior in nature on the night of Duncan's murder.

3. In the appearance of Banquo's ghost.

4. In the apparitions with their prophecies.

5. In the "air-drawn" dagger that guides Macbeth towards his victim.

The *apparitions* in Act IV, Scene 1, deserve special comment. Their three prophecies parallel the three of the first of the play. The first apparition, the helmeted head, represents Macbeth himself and echoes Macbeth's fears concerning Macduff. The second, the bloody child, represents Macduff and gives Macbeth the assurance that he must have felt in his own power—no man of woman born would ever conquer him.

Macduff's birth was of course unnatural. The third apparition, a crowned child bearing a tree, represents Malcolm, and here too the apparition just echoes the confidence Macbeth had in his own power. The apparition told Macbeth that he would never be harmed until Birnam Wood would come to Dunsinane Hill.

In each case Macbeth's interpretation is the product of his wish. Had he been less frenzied, less arrogant, he might have been warned about the possible equivocal (double) interpretation and would not have been led by overconfidence to his destruction.

The prophecies at the beginning of the play led him to his success; those at the end, to his death.

In addition to the apparitions, Banquo's ghost makes another appearance with his show of kings. The genealogical table will reveal the identity of the eight kings shown. They are Robert II and Robert III and the six Jameses terminating with James VI of Scotland and James I of England.

As has been noted, Mary Queen of Scots is omitted. This was a tactful omission by Shakespeare since James I had done nothing to save his mother from execution and came to the throne only after her death.

Most interesting of all supernatural elements are the *witches:*

1. They are closely associated with the number three and its multiples which were supposed to have magic significance.

2. Their powers were, in part (a) to foretell future events; (b) to create tempest and storms; (c) to sink ships; (d) to ride on the blast; (e) to sail the sea in a sieve.

3. They could not, however, do fatal harm to their victims if the victims did not renounce God. Hence we gather that the sailor's wife (Act I, Sc. 3) was a devout woman and the witch could revenge herself only by persecuting the husband.

4. In appearance they were sexless. Banquo says that they should be women but that they have a beard. He also tells us they are withered, their attire is wild and careless, their hands are coarse and rough, "choppy finger," and their lips thin and colorless, "skinny."

5. *Their Relation to Macbeth*—(a) Their symbolic value is that they represent Macbeth's evil ambitions. (b) Banquo sees them in Scene 3 because at that time he, too, had unworthy ambitions. Not so ambitious as Macbeth he is content with the promise that his descendants will rule Scotland. Macbeth's ambition is more immediate. (c) After Act I, Scene 3, the witches are seen by no one but Macbeth. Lennox does not see them when they leave the cavern (Act IV, Sc. 2). (d) In the latter part of the play they lead him to his destruction. But they are only manifestations of his own growing arrogance and in-

creating fury. They do not guide Macbeth, they only represent his own wishes and his own thoughts.

6. *Their Reality*—(a) Banquo saw them. (b) They would appear real and believable enough in Shakespeare's day when there was universal belief in witchcraft. James I fancied himself as an authority on witchcraft and wrote several books and pamphlets on the subject. Shakespeare flattered James by using his writings as source material.

7. *Their Unreality*—After Banquo has seen them, they appear visible to no one except Macbeth. Macbeth sees visions and images visible to no one else, e.g., the "air-drawn dagger" and Banquo's ghost. Hence it might be deduced that the witches are just another creation of his overheated brain.

8. *Hecate*—(a) Here called the Queen of the Witches. (b) Associated in mythology with Diana the goddess of the moon and the night. (c) She was supposed to preside over all nocturnal horrors.

Shakespeare's Poetry
1. His plays are written in blank verse and therefore do not rhyme. Each line contains ten syllables divided into five feet of two syllables each. The accent usually falls on the second syllable. This rhythm is known as iambic pentameter.

EXAMPLE
   "They *are*/not *yet*/come *back*./ But *I*/have *spoke*."

2. He has two devices which he uses most to avoid monotony. The first device is to alter the rhythm—which he does not hesitate to do whenever the meaning or spirit of a speech can be highlighted.

EXAMPLE
   Lady Macbeth—"Did not you speak?"
   Macbeth—"When?"
   Lady Macbeth—"Now."
   Macbeth—"As I descended?"
   Lady Macbeth—"Ay."
   Macbeth—"Hark!
      Who lies i' the second chamber?"
   Lady Macbeth—"Donalbain."

In this scene the short, terse speech reveals their true excitement.

3. His second device is (a) the run-over line or (b) the short line. In the run-over line there are more than ten syllables—usually eleven—so that the rhythm of the last syllable carries right on into the first syl-

75

lable of the next line and gives the passage a smooth continuous flow.

EXAMPLE
    (a) "That *ve*/ry *frank*/ly *he*/con*fess'd*/his *trea*/sons"
    (b) "Where*to*/the *rat*/her *shall*/his *days*/hard *jour*/ney"

The shorter line is used more sparingly and only for special effects. For example, in Act I, Scene 2, at the end of the Sergeant's speech when he is laboring under pain his last two lines become shorter, e.g.,

    "Or mem/orize/anoth/er Golgo/tha.
     I can/not tell—"

Shakespeare in his play uses rhyme for two purposes: (1) to give emphasis to those lines in which the speaker expresses a purpose or decision (2) more frequently, to mark the closing of a scene.

Rhyming occurs more frequently in his earlier plays. But he discarded it because it made the rhythm of his lines too jerky, unnatural and unlifelike.

Rhyming is almost completely absent in his most mature plays.

The Witches: To show that they were not human they were made to speak in a different rhythm. It is trochaic tetrameter—4 feet of two syllables with the accent coming upon the first syllable of each pair. Frequently, however, a syllable is lacking in the last foot.

When shall/*we* three/*meet* a/gain?
Sleep shall/*nei*ther/*night* nor/*day*.

Hecate is given the iambic rhythm with four feet to each line—iambic tetrameter. This is to show her superior rank to the witches.

    "And *I*/the *mis*/tress *of*/your *charms*."

Prose

Prose is used to either heighten or lower the dramatic pitch. In the play *Macbeth* the Porter speaks in prose because Shakespeare makes all his common people speak in prose to differentiate them from the important people in the play and from the nobility. Much low humor is written in prose.

Macbeth's letter to his wife is written in prose to set it off as a letter from the rest of the play.

In the sleep-walking scene Lady Macbeth is made to speak in prose because in that way—by contrast with her usual speech—she is able to show the strain of her emotion. In this case the dramatic pitch is heightened.

Shakespeare's poetry contains the charm and beauty of his imagery. Imagery is the ability to create images or pictures in the mind of the audience. Shakespeare's imagery is vivid and compact. Its vividness and compactness frequently are in direct ratio to the intensity of the emotional content of the lines.

For vivid imagery we can refer to Macbeth's explanation for killing the grooms (Act III, Sc. 3, 92-102).

Or again Act II, Sc. 3, 100-101:

> "The wine of life is drawn, and the mere lees
> Is left this vault to brag of."

A good example of intensity of emotion showing itself in the imagery used comes in Act I, Sc. 7, 25-28:

> "I have no spur
> To prick the sides of my intent, but only
> Vaulting ambition, which o'erleaps itself
> And falls on the other."

In Macbeth's excited mind the thoughts and emotions are coming so fast that his imagery doubles itself into a picture of spurring and of overleaping, both at the same time.

Dramatic Structure of *Macbeth*

The play is one of Shakespeare's best in symmetrical development. It has no complicating subplots; every incident and every speech is directly bound up with the central personality.

The climax of the play is reached in almost the perfect physical middle of the play and the two combine to form a satisfactory isosceles of development and denouement.

The introduction of the play takes in the first two scenes. The rising action of the play, the second part, begins with Macbeth's meeting the witches and continues until the climax—the third part—is reached in the murder of Banquo in the third scene of the third act. The fourth part, the falling action, begins with the escape of Fleance and continues on through the banquet scene, the arousing of Macduff and the retreat to Dunsinane. The fifth and final part, the conclusion, continues the falling action right up to the catastrophe that engulfs both Lady Macbeth and Macbeth.

Genealogical Tables

James I's Descent From Banquo

Banquo
>Fleance married a daughter of the Prince of Wales
>Walter Steward—Lord Steward of Scotland
>Alane Steward
>Alexander Steward
>John Steward
>Walter Steward
>Robert II, King of Scotland
>Robert III
>James I
>James II

James III
James IV married Margaret, daughter of Henry VII
James V
Mary Queen of Scots married Lord Darnley
James VI of Scotland and James I of England

Relationship Between Duncan and Macbeth

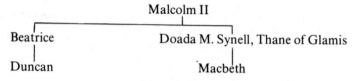

Malcolm II

Beatrice   Doada M. Synell, Thane of Glamis

Duncan   Macbeth

The Weird Sisters

"A positive decision out of demonology about the nature of the Weird Sisters seems impossible."[1] This opinion by a scholar who has devoted much time to studying the supernatural in Shakespeare may not indeed dispose of the problem for all time, but it suggests that we use some caution in our statements about Shakespeare's intention in depicting the Witches. It is also proper to remember that Holinshed was uncertain about them: "three women in strange and wild apparel, resembling creatures of [an] elder world . . . either the weird sisters, that is (as ye would say) the goddesses of destinie, or else some nymphs or feiries, indued with knowledge of prophesie by their necromanticall science . . ." (*fairies* here has its usual medieval connotation of 'diabolical spirits,' 'demons').

Holinshed's words allow for two possible interpretations: The Weird Sisters are either (1) the Three Fates or (2) devils appearing in the shapes of old women. Another quite obvious possibility is that (3) they are sorcerers. Let us briefly examine each of these alternatives.

(1) The expression *weird sisters,* which had some currency especially in North Britain at least after 1400, means, etymologically, 'Fatal' Sisters. In Old English *Wyrd* was a noun meaning 'Fate.' In ancient Germanic culture Fate was an impersonal, omnipotent power controlling all things. Its agents were three goddesses, like old women, the Norns; they ruled Past, Present, and Future. It is perhaps rather unlikely that Shakespeare knew any more about the Norns than he learned from the words of Holinshed just quoted (the spelling *weyard* or *weyward,* used several times in the Folio, may be just Shakespeare's variant of *weird*). But regardless of Shakespeare's knowledge of the Norns, the critics (like G. L. Kittredge) who understand the Sisters to be the Fates have to reckon with two major objections: (a) Shakespeare has provided the Sisters with the traditional accompaniments and attitudes of ordinary witches, for

1. R. H. West, "Night's Black Agents in Macbeth," *The Shakespeare Newsletter,* VI (1956), p. 23.

instance, with obscene beasts like toads and rats and with feelings of virulent malice; and (b)—an all-important matter—if the Norns foretell Macbeth's and Banquo's future as something that must happen inescapably, they imply that Macbeth is merely the creature of destiny and has no true volition and therefore little or no moral responsibility for his crimes. However, the importance of Macbeth's moral degeneration in this tragedy can hardly be overstated. How can the degeneration be accounted for except as the result of the hero's trying to ignore his moral responsibility? Responsibility, based on freedom of the human will, is commonly postulated as fundamental to tragedy.

Therefore, the view that the Sisters are Norns inevitably opposes the tragic meaning of the play to some degree, a result that one may assume is contrary to Shakespeare's intention.

(2) Some have thought the Sisters to be merely devils appearing as old hags (for instance, this is the view of W. C. Curry).[2] In effect, this is probably what Holinshed or his predecessors meant by calling them *fairies* and mentioning their ability to prophesy. It was generally known in Shakespeare's age that the devil, though he has no absolute knowledge of future events, can make vastly more true and specific guesses about future happenings than human beings can, particularly with reference to certain persons whose natures he knows better than they know themselves The devil's much greater knowledge of natural laws and his exhaustive memory of human history combine to give his forecasts much accuracy, compared to human predictions. And he often has much personal interest in working to make his prophecies come true, by means of temptation.

In this view of the Weird Sisters, Satan and his fellows adopt the forms of village witches in order to avoid frightening Macbeth and Banquo by some unusual and dreadful manifestation (such as that of a ghost, for instance, the dead Thane of Cawdor), yet at the same time to convince the generals of the presence of a supernatural power. Kittredge would probably object that the sight of village witches, believed to be true sorcerers, should have been a warning to the two men of the danger of dealing with Hell's agents. In fact, Banquo speaks of this danger, Act I, Sc. 3, 126:

> ... Oftentimes, to win us to our harm,
> The instruments of darkness tell us truths,
> With honest trifles, to betray's
> In deepest consequence.

But the sudden disappearance of the Witches leaves Banquo, at least, wondering whether he has not merely had an hallucination:

> ... Have we eaten on the insane root
> That takes the reason prisoner? (84-85)

2. *Shakespeare's Philosophical Patterns*, p. 79.

The display of superhuman power should have caused both men to distrust the source of the prophecies. But the devil relies successfully on the seductive appeal of the predictions, so that even Banquo is impelled to ask for a prophecy for himself; it is only later that he asks, *What? Can the devil speak true?* (107). Macbeth's soliloquy, Act I, Sc. 3, 130-142, may be, as R. M. Frye asserts, a deliberate attempt to avoid admitting to himself the evil source of the predictions in order thus to evade a moral choice.[3] It is almost certain that the Elizabethan audience believed Macbeth guilty of mortal sin in his willingness to take pleasure in the Witches' predictions—not because of their substance, but because they come from Satan.

(3) The Witches may simply be sorcerers, that is, ordinary witches as understood in the sixteenth century. That there are persons who deal directly and consciously with the devil and thus damn themselves, in order to obtain superhuman power, is the doctrine of King James's *Demonologie,* and of course it was orthodox Protestant and Catholic belief. However, by no means all professed Christians believed that the witches who were prosecuted, especially in rural places, were real sorcerers; the argument that most village witches were just deluded or senile people was commonplace in the controversy over witchcraft which was one feature of European intellectual life at the end of the sixteenth century, and of which the *Demonologie* is a part. We probably have no way of determining how many persons in the Globe audience were convinced that witchcraft was common. But it is certainly not extravagant to say that at least three-quarters of the audience must have believed that witchcraft does occur, whether commonly or not.

This view, (3), presents essentially the same moral and tragic implications about Macbeth's career as does (2). For the Weird Sisters, if they are true witches, have sold themselves to the devil and therefore act as his agents in deluding Macbeth to crimes that will ultimately damn his soul to their company in Hell. Hence, they are as malignant as devils and rejoice in destruction as do their masters.

To draw the distinction between real witches and devils appearing as witches is to imply that there are, or should be, some means of determining which of the two Shakespeare intended. But because the dramatist and his audience knew that the devil is the father of lies and deceit, even the following lines may not finally solve the problem:

> *1 Witch.*   Say, if thou'dst rather hear it from our mouths,
> Or from our masters'?
> *Macbeth*   Call 'em; let me see 'em. (Act IV, Sc. 1, 62-63)

Whereupon the apparitions rise from Hell. Presumably the apparitions are really devils, the Witches are not. Perhaps the Elizabethan view, and the one we should adopt, is implied in the First Witch's question as well as in the fact that Hecate (a character possibly

3.   *Shakespeare and Christian Doctrine,* p. 258.

intruded into the play by someone other than Shakespeare) calls the Sisters *beldams,* not demons (Act III, Sc. 5, 2).

Macbeth's Motivation

Ambition in Elizabethan English denotes aspiration for power, but connotes always that the aspiration is evil. In our country, to aspire to political power is laudable, for the power that is sought is delegated by the people only to one who they think has proved himself worthy of it. But for an Elizabethan or Scottish gentleman to aspire to be king would imply a willingness or desire to break the divine order in society (in particular, the order of succession to the throne) and to take the power from one for whom Providence had designed it. Macbeth, therefore, has been guilty of the sin of ambition before the Witches first speak to him; Lady Macbeth testifies to this fact, Act I, Sc. 5, 18-20. He is punished for the sin, but much more for its great consequences, his acts of murder, usurpation, and tyranny. However, if you mention in an examination that Macbeth is punished for ambition, realize that you are using the word in the Elizabethan sense—and also that you are telling a very small part of the truth. For murder, usurpation, and cruelty are public *crimes,* whereas ambition (as 'illicit aspiration for power') remains a private *sin,* no matter how grievous. The misery that crushes Macbeth is due to his crimes. His ambition only makes him a menace to society.

As to his indifference to supernatural punishment: The critics are not agreed on the kind of moral scruples that Macbeth feels before killing Duncan and the kind of anguish that he afterward suffers for this and his other murders. Sir Herbert Grierson says: "He may profess contempt of moral scruples and supernatural inhibitions, and declare that if he were safe in this world he would 'jump the life to come.' The voices that he hears and the visions that he sees give him the lie."[1] And Bradley more concisely expresses the same idea: "His conscious or reflective mind . . . moves chiefly among considerations of outward success and failure, while his inner being is convulsed by conscience."[2]

On the other hand, Roland M. Frye believes that Shakespeare does not, either here or elsewhere, focus upon rewards and punishments in the after life, as do Bunyan and Milton, for instance. "That Macbeth degenerated into a viciously evil man, there can be no doubt, and it is also true that we can trace in his degeneration the patterns of the course of sin which the theologians taught." But, "though Shakespeare gives dramatic acknowledgement to that eternal judgment [the reward of either Heaven or Hell], his concern in the plays is for judgments which are passed upon evil in this life . . . his focus remains upon the temporal operation of the devil's kingdom."[3] These different opinions may perhaps be reconciled

1. Quoted by Muir, *Macbeth,* p. lvi.
2. *Ibid.*
3. *Shakespeare and Christian Doctrine,* (1963), pp. 150-152, 144.

by saying that Macbeth does not speak of eternal punishment after death (except to say he will *jump* ['risk'] *the life to come,* Act I, Sc. 7, 7), and therefore he appears to ignore or forget it; but he suffers from the guilt and horror of his crimes as only a man could who had kept alive in his soul a keen sense of his dependence on God through religion—and this would imply a remembrance of eternal destiny. Certainly a religious person will interpret Macbeth's anguish in this way; and most of the original audience of *Macbeth* were formally and more or less sincerely religious.

No doubt Shakespeare thought that to try to reveal Macbeth's punishment as an agonized fear of damnation would be a task for a lyric or narrative poet, not for a dramatist. In the theatre the criminal's sense of isolation from mankind, of universal hatred towards him, of danger of attack, of the power of the devil over him, of loss of comradeship with his wife—all these are much more ready, familiar media to express the beginnings of damnation as they are felt in this world.

Banquo's Silence About Macbeth's Crime

The primary reason why some critics have found Banquo's silence about the murder of Duncan disturbing to them is that Shakespeare has been at pains to depict Banquo as a remarkably virtuous and attractive man. His valor and leadership have scarcely been excelled by Macbeth's own. Says Duncan,

> Noble Banquo,
> Thou hast no less deserv'd, nor must be known
> No less to have done so. (Act I, Sc. 4, 29-31)

Banquo is generous in praise of Macbeth (Act I, Sc. 4, 54-55), loyal to his King (Act II, Sc. 1, 26-31), candid (Act II, Sc. 3, 136-158). Although the fact is extraneous to the play, we might also remember that he was King James's ancestor, and the playwright will prefer not to show him in any base act.

Yet the good Banquo, strongly suspecting that Macbeth has killed Duncan, says nothing publicly against the usurper. What explanation can be made of this acquiescence in Macbeth's crime? It is possible that no wholly satisfying reason can be offered; but we must take note of certain important elements of the situation.

First, we are dealing with a rapidly moving play, a fact never to be forgotten. After the stupifying discovery of Duncan's body, Banquo, like the other thanes, is bewildered at first. He proclaims his own innocence of any knowledge of a plot and his determination to oppose further treason:

> In the great hand of God I stand, and thence
> Against the undivulg'd ['undiscovered'] pretence
>   ['intention'] I fight
> Of treason malice. (Act II, Sc. 3, 136-138)

All retire to prepare for the great council of state, and meanwhile Malcolm and Donalbain seem to establish their own guilt by secretly fleeing from Scotland. A short scene follows which reveals Macduff's suspicions of everyone, next day; but Shakespeare withdraws Banquo from the scene quite clearly to avoid the dramatic difficulty of Banquo's having to begin to suspect Macbeth by the time of the council. The plan of the play requires that Macbeth shall be elected without a conflict. In the next scene, some time later, we meet Banquo again; in soliloquy he voices his suspicions that Macbeth was the murderer.

Now, several things are to be noted here: (1) Macduff, in the preceding scene, is "in a mood of universal suspicion," and therefore he is not distinguished for us as one *who already fully understands what has happened.* And for this reason we do not assume that Banquo, either, begins immediately to suspect Macbeth. The flight of the two Princes is a plot-device of great importance here, for it misleads all Scotsmen, including Banquo, for a little while. (2) By the time Banquo can conceive the idea that Macbeth may be guilty, the usurper has been crowned by consent of the council. To charge the King with murder is now a momentous undertaking. (3) In the theatre we are indeed aware that Banquo heard the prophecy of Macbeth's being king hereafter. But that Macbeth, the valiant, loyal kinsman of Duncan, could murder his benefactor is so preposterous an idea that only because we almost witnessed the crime can we accuse Banquo of being slow to realize Macbeth's guilt.

And now that Macbeth is actually King, and the true heir to the throne has fled far away, Banquo does not disclose his suspicions or attempt to raise an insurrection. First of all, we must allow some weight to the doctrine of passive obedience. In Tudor doctrine any resistance to the sovereign is a grave sin. Macbeth is the anointed King and by blood has a claim to the sovereignty. Banquo may well reflect, "Let me wait until some definite evidence of Macbeth's crime becomes public or until Malcolm leads an invasion to recover his right. Can I begin a rebellion merely on suspicion of Macbeth's guilt? Unjust conspiracy against the King is dreadful treason." It is true that Banquo also thinks exultantly of the prediction that his seed shall be kings ultimately. But note that that thought might as well inspire him to rebel as to remain silent; therefore, his hope of his children's succession is not a dramatic cause of his acquiescence in Macbeth's sovereignty. Finally, the change of Macbeth's character to that of a bloody tyrant has not yet been shown to the world— naturally, Banquo is unaware that he himself is to be first victim of the radical change in Macbeth.

All in all, we cannot much blame Banquo for his initial bewilderment and later hesitation.

Shakespeare's Imagery in *Macbeth*

The imagery in *Macbeth* appears to me to be more rich and varied, more highly imaginative, more unapproachable by any other writer, than that of any other single play. It is particularly so, I think, in the continuous use made of the simplest, humblest, everyday things, drawn from the daily life in a small house, as a vehicle for sublime poetry. But that is beside our point here.

The ideas in the imagery are in themselves more imaginative, more subtle and complex than in other plays, and there are a greater number of them, interwoven the one with the other, recurring and repeating. There are at least four of these main ideas, and many subsidiary ones.

One is the picture of Macbeth himself.

Few simple things—harmless in themselves—have such a curiously humiliating and degrading effect as the spectacle of a notably small man enveloped in a coat far too big for him. Comic actors know this well— Charlie Chaplin, for instance—and it is by means of this homely picture that Shakespeare shows us his imaginative view of the hero, and expresses the fact that the honours for which the murders were committed are, after all, of very little worth to him.

The idea constantly recurs that Macbeth's new honours sit ill upon him, like a loose and badly fitting garment, belonging to someone else. Macbeth himself first expresses it, quite early in the play, when, immediately following the first appearance of the witches and their prophecies, Ross arrives from the king, and greets him as thane of Cawdor, to which Macbeth quickly replies.

The thane of Cawdor lives: why do you dress me
In borrow'd robes?   (Act I, Sc. 3, 108)

And a few minutes later, when he is rapt in ambitious thoughts suggested by the confirmation of two out of the three "prophetic greetings," Banquo, watching him, murmurs,

New honours come upon him,
Like our strange garments, cleave not to their mould
But with the aid of use.   (Act I, Sc. 3, 144)

When Duncan is safely in the castle, Macbeth's better nature for a moment asserts itself, and, in debate with himself, he revolts from the contemplated deed for a threefold reason: because of its incalculable results, the treachery of such action from one who is both kinsman and host, and Duncan's own virtues and greatness as king.

When his wife joins him, his repugnance to the deed is as great, but it is significant that he gives three quite different reasons for not going ahead with it, reasons which he hopes may appeal to her, for he knows the others would not. So he urges that he has been lately honoured by the king, people think well of him, and therefore he should reap the reward of these things at once, and not upset everything by this murder which they have planned.

There is irony in the fact that to express the position he uses the same metaphor of clothes:

> I have bought
> Golden opinions from all sorts of people,
> Which would be worn now in their newest gloss,
> Not cast aside so soon.   (Act I, Sc. 7, 32)

To which Lady Macbeth, quite unmoved, retorts contemptuously:

> Was the hope drunk
> Wherein you dress'd yourself?   (Act I, Sc. 7, 36)

After the murder, when Ross says he is going to Scone for Macbeth's coronation, Macduff uses the same simile:

> Well, may you see things well done there: adieu!
> Lest our old robes sit easier than our new!   (Act II, Sc. 4, 37)

And, at the end, when the tyrant is at bay at Dunsinane, and the English troops are advancing, the Scottish lords still have this image in their minds. Caithness sees him as a man vainly trying to fasten a large garment on him with too small a belt:

> He cannot buckle his distemper'd cause
> Within the belt of rule;   (Act V, Sc. 2, 15)

while Angus, in a similar image, vividly sums up the essence of what they all have been thinking ever since Macbeth's accession to power:

> now does he feel his title
> Hang loose about him, like a giant's robe
> Upon a dwarfish thief.   (Act V, Sc. 2, 20)

This imaginative picture of a small, ignoble man encumbered and degraded by garments unsuited to him, should be put against the view emphasised by some critics (notably Coleridge and Bradley) of the likeness between Macbeth and Milton's Satan in grandeur and sublimity.

Undoubtedly Macbeth is built on great lines and in heroic proportions, with great possibilities—there could be no tragedy else. He is great, magnificently great, in courage, in passionate, indomitable ambition, in imagination and capacity to feel. But he could never be put beside, say Hamlet or Othello, in nobility of nature; and there is an aspect in which he is but a poor, vain, cruel, treacherous creature, snatching ruthlessly over the dead bodies of kinsman and friend at place and power he is utterly unfitted to possess. It is worth remembering that it is thus that Shakespeare, with his unshrinking clarity of vision, repeatedly *sees* him.

Another image or idea which runs through *Macbeth* is the reverberation of sound echoing over vast regions, even into the limitless spaces beyond the confines of the world. Echoing sound, as also reflected light, always interested Shakespeare; he is very quick to notice it, and in the earlier plays he records it often, quite simply and directly, as in the reverberating roll of drums in *King John,* the smack of Petruchio's kiss resounding through the church, Juliet's delicate picture of Echo with her airy tongue repeating "Romeo," Viola's assertion that were she Orsino, she would make the

> babbling gossip of the air
> Cry out "Olivia!"   (*Twelfth Night,* Act I, Sc. 5, 283)

or her more fanciful remark to the duke that the tune he likes

> gives a very echo to the seat
> Where love is throned.   (Act II, Sc. 4, 21)

He specially loves, and describes repeatedly (in *A Midsummer Night's Dream, Titus Andronicus* and the *Taming of the Shrew*), the re-echoing sound of hounds and horn,

> the musical confusion
> Of hounds and echo in conjunction;
> (*Midsummer Night's Dream,* Act IV, Sc. 1, 115)

its doubling and mocking quality attracts him:

> the babbling echo mocks the hounds,
> Replying shrilly to the well-tuned horns,
> As if a double hunt were heard at once;
> (*Titus Andronicus,* Act II, Sc. 3, 17)

and it is this quality which Warwick applies most appositely when, having been roused in the small hours to soothe the sleepless and fretful king, he finally loses patience with Henry's fears that the revolutionaries must be fifty thousand strong, and retorts, somewhat tartly,

> It cannot be, my lord;
> Rumour doth double, like the voice and echo,
> The numbers of the fear'd. Please it your grace
> To go to bed.   (*Henry IV, Part II,* Act III, Sc. 1, 96)

It is not until after 1600, and most noticeably in *Troilus and Cressida,* that Shakespeare uses this same idea of reverberation and reflection to illustrate subtle and philosophic thought. Ulysses' mind is full of it, and he applies it constantly; Kent, in *King Lear* (Act I, Sc. 1, 155), seizes on an analogous natural fact to point the truth that noise and protestation do not necessarily indicate deep feeling; while in *Macbeth,* the peculiar quality of echoing and re-echoing sound is used to emphasise, in the most highly imaginative and impressive way, a thought constantly present with

Shakespeare in his middle years, the incalculable and boundless effects of evil in the nature of one man.

Macbeth himself, like Hamlet, is fully conscious of how impossible it is to "trammel up the consequence" of his deed, and by his magnificent images of angels pleading trumpet-tongued,

> And pity, like a naked, new-born babe,
> Striding the blast, or heaven's cherubin horsed
> **Upon the sightless couriers of the air,**   (Act I, Sc. 7, 21)
"Who"
> **Shall blow the horrid deed in every eye,**
> That tears shall drown the wind,   (Act I, Sc. 7, 24)

he fills our imagination with the picture of its being broadcast through great spaces with reverberating sound.

This is taken up again by Macduff, when he cries,

> each new morn
> New widows howl, new orphans cry, new sorrows
> Strike heaven on the face, that it resounds
> As if it felt with Scotland and yell'd out
> Like syllable of dolour;   (Act IV, Sc. 3, 4)

and again by Ross, when he is trying to break the terrible news of Macbeth's latest murders to Macduff—the destruction of his own wife and children—

> I have words
> That would be howl'd out in the desert air,
> Where hearing should not latch them.
>
> (Act IV, Sc. 3, 193)

One can scarcely conceive a more vivid picture of the vastnesses of space than this, and of the overwhelming and unending nature of the consequences or reverberations of the evil deed.

Another constant idea in the play arises out of the symbolism that light stands for life, virtue, goodness; and darkness for evil and death. "Angels are bright" (Act IV, Sc. 3, 22), the witches are "secret, black and midnight hags" (Act IV, Sc. 1, 48), and, as Dowden says, the movement of the whole play might be summed up in the words, "good things of day begin to droop and drowse" (Act III, Sc. 2, 52).

This is, of course, very obvious, but out of it develops the further thought which is assumed throughout, that the evil which is being done is so horrible that it would blast the sight to look on it; so that darkness, or partial blinding, is necessary to carry it out.

Like so much in the play it is ironic that it should be Duncan who first starts this simile, the idea of which turns into a leading motive in the tragedy. When he is conferring the new honour on his son, he is careful to say that others, kinsmen and thanes, will also be rewarded:

> signs of nobleness, like stars, shall shine
> On all deservers. (Act I, Sc. 4, 41)

No sooner has the king spoken, than Macbeth realises that Malcolm, now a prince of the realm, is an added obstacle in his path, and suddenly, shrinking from the blazing horror of the murderous thought which follows, he cries to himself,

> Stars, hide your fires;
> Let not light see my black and deep desires.
>
> (Act I, Sc. 4, 50)

From now on, the idea that only in darkness can such evil deeds be done is ever present with both Macbeth and his wife, as is seen in their two different and most characteristic invocations to darkness: her blood-curdling cry.

> Come, thick night,
> And pall thee in the dunnest smoke of hell,
>
> (Act I, Sc. 5, 51)

which takes added force when we hear later the poignant words. "She has light by her continually" (Act V, Sc. 1, 23); and his more gentle appeal in the language of falconry,

> Come, seeling night,
> Scarf up the tender eyes of pitiful day.
>
> (Act III, Sc. 2, 46)

And when Banquo, sleepless, uneasy, with heart heavy as lead, crosses the courtyard on the fateful night, with Fleance holding the flaring torch before him, and, looking up to the dark sky, mutters,

> There's husbandry in heaven,
> Their candles are all out,   (Act II, Sc. 1, 4)

we know the scene is set for treachery and murder.

So it is fitting that on the day following, "dark night strangles the travelling lamp" (Act II, Sc. 4, 7), and

> darkness does the face of earth entomb,
> When living light should kiss it.   (Act II, Sc. 4, 9)

The idea of deeds which are too terrible for human eyes to look on is also constant; Lady Macbeth scoffs it—"the sleeping and the dead," she argues, "are but as pictures" (Act II, Sc. 2, 53):

> 'tis the eye of childhood
> That fears a painted devil;

but Macduff, having seen the slain King, rushes out, and cries to Lennox,

> Approach the chamber, and destroy your sight
> With a new Gorgon.   (Act II, Sc. 3, 76)

Macbeth boldly asserts he dare look on that "which might appal the devil" (Act III, Sc. 4, 60), and the bitterness of defeat he realises on seeing one "too like the spirit of Banquo" in the procession of kings, is expressed in his agonised cry,

> Thy crown does sear mine eye-balls; (Act IV, Sc. 1, 113)

while in his bitter and beautiful words at the close, the dominant thoughts and images are the quenching of light and the empty reverberation of sound and fury, "signifying nothing" (Act V, Sc. 5, 28).

The fourth of the chief symbolic ideas in the play is one which is very constant with Shakespeare, and is to be found all through his work, that sin is a disease—Scotland is sick.

So Macbeth, while repudiating physic for himself, turns to the doctor and says if he could, by analysis, find Scotland's disease

> And purge it to a sound and pristine health,
> I would applaud thee to the very echo.
> That should applaud again . . .
> What rhubarb, senna, or what purgative drug,
> Would scour these English hence?   (Act V, Sc. 3, 52)

Malcolm speaks of his country as weeping, bleeding and wounded, and later urges Macduff to

> make us medicines of our great revenge,
> To cure this deadly grief;   (Act IV, Sc. 3, 214)

while Caithness calls Malcolm himself the "medicine of the sickly weal," "the country's purge" (Act V, Sc. 2, 27). It is worth noting that all Macbeth's images of sickness are remedial or soothing in character: balm for a sore, sleep after fever, a purge, physic for pain, a "sweet oblivious antidote" (Act V, Sc. 3, 43); thus intensifying to the reader or audience his passionate and constant longing for well-being, rest, and, above all, peace of mind.

Other subsidiary motives in the imagery, which work in and out through the play, insensibly but deeply affect the reader's imagination. One of these is the idea of the *unnaturalness* of Macbeth's crime, that it is a convulsion of nature. This is brought out repeatedly and emphasised by imagery, as are also the terrible results of going against nature.

Macbeth himself says that Duncan's wounds

> look'd like a breach in nature
> For ruin's wasteful entrance,   (Act II, Sc. 3, 118)

and Macduff speaks of his murder as the sacrilege of breaking open the Lord's anointed temple (Act II, Sc. 3, 71). The events which accompany and follow it are terrible because unnatural; an owl kills a falcon, horses eat each other, the earth was feverous and did shake, day becomes night; all this, says the old man, is unnatural,

> Even like the deed that's done.   (Act II, Sc. 4, 10)

Macbeth's greatest trouble is the unnatural one that he has murdered sleep (Act II, Sc. 2, 36), and the whole feeling of dislocation is increased by such images as "let the frame of things disjoint" (Act III, Sc. 2, 16), or by Macbeth's conjuration to the witches with the terrible list of the convulsions of nature which may result from their answering him. Indeed, if from one angle the movement of the play may be summed up in Macbeth's words,

> Good things of day begin to droop and drowse.   (Act III, Sc. 2, 52)

from another it is completely described by the doctor in his diagnosis of the doomed queen's malady as "a great perturbation in nature" (Act V, Sc. 1, 10).

In addition to these running images symbolising or expressing an idea, there are groups of others which might be called atmospheric in their effect, that is, they raise or increase certain feelings and emotions.

Such is the action of rapid riding, which contributes and emphasises a certain sense of rushing, relentless and goaded motion, of which we are very conscious in the play. This is symbolised externally by the rapid ride of the messenger to Lady Macbeth, arriving "almost dead for breath," ahead of Macbeth, who himself has outridden Duncan (Act I, Sc. 5, 37). The king remarks in unconscious irony,

> he rides well,
> And his great love, sharp as his spur, hath holp him
> To his home before us.   (Act I, Sc. 6, 22)

It is noticeable what a large part riding plays in the images which crowd on Macbeth's heated brain when he is weighing the *pros* and *cons* of his plan (Act I, Sc. 7, 1-28): the new-born babe "striding the blast," heaven's cherubin horsed

> Upon the sightless couriers of the air,   (Act I, Sc. 7, 23)

and finally, the vision of his "intent," his aim, as a horse lacking sufficient spur to action, which melts into the picture of his ambition as a rider vaulting into the saddle with such energy that it "o'erleaps itself," and falls on the further side.

The feeling of fear, horror and pain is increased by the constant and recurring images of blood, these are very marked, and have been noticed by others, especially by Bradley, the most terrible being Macbeth's description of himself wading in a river of blood, (Act III, Sc. 4, 136); while the most stirring to the imagination, perhaps in the whole of Shakespeare, is the picture of him gazing, rigid with horror, at his own blood-stained hand and watching it dye the whole green ocean red (Act II, Sc. 2, 60).

The images of animals also, nearly all predatory, unpleasant or fierce, add to this same feeling; such are a nest of scorpions, a venomous serpent and a snake, a "hell-kite" eating chickens, a devouring vulture, a swarm of insects, a tiger, rhinoceros and bear, the tiny wren fighting the owl for the life of her young, small birds with the fear of the net, lime, pitfall or gin, used with such bitter ironic effect by Lady Macduff and her boys just before they are murdered, the shrieking owl, and the bear tied to a stake fighting savagely to the end.

Enough has been said, I think, to indicate how complex and varied is the symbolism in the imagery of *Macbeth,* and to make it clear that an appreciable part of the emotions we feel throughout of pity, fear and horror, is due to the subtle but definite and repeated action of this imagery upon our minds, of which, in our preoccupation with the main theme, we remain often largely unconscious.

By Caroline F.E. Spurgeon

Selected Criticisms

Viewed superficially, *Macbeth* is a drama with the theme "Crime does not pay." It is that, but it is much more than that. One of the things that make it more than that is that it is concerned with no ordinary criminals. The prize they seek is great, the temptation is unusual, the crime is most heinous, and they themselves have capacities that are in certain respects extraordinary. The distance between the delight in the exercise of power they expect and the agony they suffer is tremendous. Yet, although everything is heightened in this world of the poetic imagination, everything is convincingly real.

We feel toward them and their catastrophe more than the fascination and the awe with which we witness the extraordinary. We sympathize with them. It may seem strange to say that we identify ourselves with one who is a murderer of women and children, but it is true. Shakespeare makes us feel what it is to be a Macbeth, makes us share his terrors and his desperation. And even though the courage which had first aroused our admiration is used to enable him to continue in his course despite the tortures inflicted on him by his conscience it remains admirable, as does the strength of the conscience which he is never quite able to crush.

Even at the conclusion Macbeth never quite forfeits our complete sympathy. The memory of what he was and his own regret for the human values he has lost makes him more than the diabolical figure or the trapped animal which he is regarded as being by his opponents, although he is that too. Through him we have seen the potentialities of human nature for good and for evil. That he brought his own downfall upon himself only heightens the tragic effect, for we are aware how narrow is the margin between saving one's self and losing one's self, how terribly a part of him fought against that in him which led him to his downfall, how much he himself cast away—and yet how difficult it was for him not to do so.

We cannot, therefore, simply say, "It serves him right." His satanic defiance at the end elicits a horrified admiration. We acquiesce in the retribution which overtakes him, for, even though we identify ourselves with Macbeth, we are also able to stand outside of him and see the consequences of his action inevitably destroying him. Realizing, however, the great human qualities which have been devastated in the course of the drama, our response is a complex one that includes a sense of waste. To put it in the very simplest terms, it includes such feelings as "How awful" as well as "It had to be."

Because the hero is a criminal, *Macbeth,* one of the world's great tragedies, violates many of the critical clichés about tragedy. We are told that the tragic hero must be a good man with a flaw of character, but a man who wantonly kills women and children can scarcely be called good. We are told that the tragic hero gains a dearly earned self-knowledge, but Macbeth continues to deceive himself up to the end, thinking that one more successful murder or one more successful battle will make him happy. We are told the tragic hero's defeat is also in some sense a triumph, but it would be hard to claim that Macbeth triumphs in any way. What we can say is that, even though Macbeth is not a "good" man and even though his downfall is not a mingled triumph and defeat, we do receive from his catastrophe the sense of the glory and dignity of man which we get from the downfall of the more conventional tragic hero. We get too the kind of perception concerning him and the human situation which the hero himself in other tragedies often gets.

Because Macbeth is the kind of hero that he is, he evokes less pity than the tragic hero often does. King Lear is a majestic figure, but in the course of the tragedy we see him as a "foolish fond old man" who arouses our tenderest feelings as he learns the meaning of love from his daughter Cordelia. Othello too is a commanding person, but, as Iago brings him low, we feel that his words, "The pity of it, Iago," apply to himself as much as to Desdemona. Not so with Macbeth.

Yet the tragedy in which he appears is not devoid of pathos. It is most evident when we witness the calamities that come to the innocent victims of Macbeth. In the scene in which Lady Macduff and her son are murdered, we do not put ourselves in their places and share the terror that besets them. We look upon it as a piteous spectacle irradiated by the beauty of the mother's love and the charm of the boy's precocious cleverness. The simple, wholesome domestic feelings come as a relief from the great passions of Macbeth and Lady Macbeth.

We also, however, even feel something of pity for these two towering figures in the face of their agony and desolation, although this pity is of a grudging, sterner sort. When, as Macbeth feveredly speaks of new murders, Lady Macbeth replies wearily, "You lack the season of all natures, sleep," we appreciate her solicitude for him and perceive her own unvoiced misery. If she had dissolved into self-pity with some such statement as "If only I could get a good night's sleep!" her grandeur and that of the tragedy would have been shattered. But the implied statement and her concern for him humanizes her and evokes some pity even as her stoicism in suffering maintains her stature.

The doctor observing Lady Macbeth's sleepwalking acts as a choric guide to our response. "God, God forgive us all!" he exclaims. Predominant in these words is the feeling of horror and awe at what he has seen: "The terrible crimes of which human beings are capable! God forgive all of us for the evil within us!" But also present is a sense of pity for poor, suffering frail humanity: "The tortures which human beings can bring upon themselves! God forgive all of us, for we know not what we do until it is too late!"

For, extraordinary individuals as Macbeth and Lady Macbeth are, they are also representative of humanity. Their situation is the human situation. The evil which engulfs them is the evil which surrounds each of us. Of course, the dramatic universe that is *Macbeth* is not ordinary, everyday life in suburban North America. But it is a dramatic and poetic heightening of certain aspects of that life. All of us do things which have unforeseen consequences, and none of us can escape from the past and from ourselves. It might further be argued that *Macbeth* makes us more sharply aware of an essential reality of our time—the memory of genocide and mass slaughter, the alienation, the suppressed terror and violence— that lies beneath the placid surface of things.

This is a function of poetic drama. It presents us not with the surface of things but with a world of the imagination that has significance for us. It is important to remember that *Macbeth* is such a poetic drama. The poetry is not a mere convention or a mere ornament but the medium through which the effect is conveyed. This is why a study of its language and its poetic devices is so rewarding. These devices work their effect upon us even though we are not conscious of them. But if *Macbeth* is poetry, it is also drama. All of the images, symbols, and themes in the world would not make *Macbeth* what it is if it did not create characters who are life-like while greater than life-size. *Macbeth* is neither pure poetry nor pure drama but a poetic drama. In the theater we should not spend our time counting images, but our experience should be enriched by the close reading we have given the play.

P.N. Siegel

... *Macbeth* is a study in the complementary pair of passions of rash courage and fear. It begins with the courage that is not real courage and ends with the courage that is not real courage. It pictures in turn the military courage of Macbeth, his excited valour and excessive bravery in action, the drunken courage of Lady Macbeth, the bravery of passion, the fury of despair, and the courage of desperation. It pictures as well superstitious fear, melancholy fear, the fear of those who share our secrets, the fear of those who are our rivals, the fear of those whom we have harmed, all the fears that lead to murder after murder, that result in melancholy, in sleeplessness, in disturbing dreams, in ghosts and visions, in fits of passion, in frenzy, in sleep-walking, in self-destruction; fears that destroy peace and happiness and honour and hope; fears that make ambitions fruitless and success a mockery.

But the study is also a study of man and woman. Lady Macbeth is pictured as sinning partly, I think, in that she is false to herself as woman. She is pictured as consciously unsexing herself, as converting all that is womanly into the courage and determination to be cruel. Even more than Macbeth, she wills to do evil. She dyes her will in her ambition. Because her will is strong and directed by passion and not by reason, the fear that is her punishment is more terrible than that of Macbeth and brings her even to the despairful sin of self-destruction.

Macbeth is, however, not only a study of fear; it is a study in fear. The sounds and images in the play combine to give the atmosphere of terror and fear. The incantation of the witches, the bell that tolls while Duncan dies, the cries of Duncan, the cries of the women as Lady Macbeth dies, the owl, the knocking at the gate, the wild horses that ate each other, the storm, the quaking of the earth—all of these are the habitual accompaniments of the wilfully fearful in literature.

Lily B. Campbell

... Shakespeare in *Macbeth* probed the inner workings of a human mind. The personal ethical aspects of the play have been so vital and absorbing that critics have tended to forget that interwoven inseparably with the ethical problems are political problems with which Shakespeare was deeply concerned. As we have long known ... the play was presented before King James as a tribute to what the king considered his actual, not mythical, ancestors. *Macbeth* must have been regarded by its Jacobean audience as a depiction of legitimate history, and they must have expected to find in it the customary didactic uses of history ...

... There are many political overtones in the play, but Shakespeare is concerned primarily with two problems: the characteristics of the ideal king, and the duty of a loyal subject under a tyrant. Both of these themes come to a head in the third scene of Act IV, when Macduff visits Malcolm in England. This is the most crucial political scene of the play, one in which Shakespeare offers perhaps his final answers to questions which had concerned him throughout his career as a dramatist.

Irving Ribner

Macbeth is probably the best known and certainly the most perfectly unified of Shakespeare's tragedies. There is perhaps no Shakespearean play, unless it be *Romeo and Juliet*, of which the mere enumeration of its events is so significant, so impressive. On the ground of this universal application, it presents the spectacle of a representative man and woman embarking on a sea of sin and error and encountering a shipwreck, not only as individuals, but as husband and wife. *Macbeth* is thus a tragedy of the marriage relation as well as of the state. The joint guilt of Macbeth and Lady Macbeth ultimately separates them, and they perish as individuals, each alone.

Hardin Craig

In this vast world torn from the universe of night, there are three tragic themes. The first theme is that of the actual guilt, and the separation in damnation of the two characters—the man ... and the woman ...

The second tragic theme of the play is the man's love for the woman whose damnation is of the earth, who is unable, until death is near, to conceive of the damnation of the spirit, and who in her blindness therefore strays away from him, leaving him for ever in his lonely hell.

The third tragic theme is the woman's despairing love for the man whose vision she cannot see, and whom she has helped to drive into damnation.

Edith Sitwell

Darkness, we may even say blackness, broods over this tragedy. It is remarkable that almost all the scenes which at once recur to memory take place either at night or in some dark spot.... The blackness of night is to the hero a thing of fear, even of horror; and that which he feels becomes the spirit of the play ...

Let us observe another point. The vividness, magnitude, and violence of the imagery ... are characteristic of *Macbeth* almost throughout; and their influence contributes to form its atmosphere. Images like those of the babe torn smiling from the breast and dashed to death; of pouring the sweet milk of concord into hell; of the earth shaking in fever; ... and of the tale told by an idiot, full of sound and fury;—all keep the imagination moving on a 'wild and violent sea,' while it is scarcely for a moment permitted to dwell on thoughts of peace and beauty. In its language, as in its action, the drama is full of tumult and storm ....

... All this has one effect, to excite supernatural alarm and, even more, a dread of the presence of evil not only in its recognised seat but all through and around our mysterious nature. Perhaps there is no other work equal to *Macbeth* in the production of this effect.

A.C. Bradley

... [Macbeth] is presented as a mature man of definitely established character, successful in certain fields of activity and enjoying an enviable reputation. We must not conclude, therefore, that all his volitions and actions are predictable; Macbeth's character, like any other man's at a given moment, is what is being made out of potentialities plus environment, and no one, not even Macbeth himself, can know all his potentialitites. It is clear, however, that he is first revealed as a man of inordinate self-love whose actions are discovered to be—and no doubt have been for a long time—determined mainly by an inordinate desire for some temporal or mutable good . . . .

Macbeth is actuated in his conduct mainly by an inordinate desire for worldly honors; his delight lies primarily in buying golden opinions from all sorts of people. But we must not, therefore, deny him an entirely human complexity of motives. For example, his fighting in Duncan's service is magnificent and courageous, and his evident joy in it is traceable in part to the natural pleasure which accompanies the explosive expenditure of prodigious physical energy and the euphoria which follows. He also rejoices no doubt in the success which crowns his efforts in battle—and so on. He may even conceive of the proper motive which should energize back of his great deed:

The service and the loyalty I owe,
In doing it, pays itself.

But while he destroys the king's enemies, such motives work but dimly at best and are obscured in his consciousness by more vigorous urges. In the main, as we have said, his nature violently demands rewards: he fights valiantly in order that he may be reported in such terms as 'valour's minion' and 'Bellona's bridegroom'; he values success because it brings spectacular fame and new titles and royal favor heaped upon him in public. Now so long as these mutable goods are at all commensurate with his inordinate desires—and such is the case, up until he covets the kingship—Macbeth remains an honorable gentleman. He is not a criminal; he has no criminal tendencies. But once permit his self-love to demand a satisfaction which cannot be honorably attained, and he is likely to grasp any dishonorable means to that end which may be safely employed. In other words, Macbeth has much of *natural* good in him unimpaired; environment has conspired with his nature to make him upright in all his dealings with those about him. But *moral* goodness in him is undeveloped and indeed still rudimentary, for his voluntary acts are scarcely brought into harmony with ultimate ends . . . .

As he returns from victorious battle, puffed up with self-love which demands ever-increasing recognition of his greatness, the demonic forces of evil—symbolized by the Weird Sisters—suggest to his inordinate imagination the splendid prospect of attaining now the greatest mutable good he has ever desired. These demons in the guise of witches cannot read his inmost thoughts, but from observation of facial expression and other bodily manifestations they surmise with comparative accuracy what passions drive him and what dark desires await their fostering. Realizing that he wishes the kingdom, they prophesy that he shall be king. They cannot thus compel his will to evil; but they do arouse his passions and stir up a vehement and inordinate apprehension of the imagination, which so perverts the judgment of reason that it leads his will toward choosing means to the desired temporal good. Indeed his imagination and passions are so vivid under this evil impulse from without that 'nothing is but what is not'; and his reason is so impeded that he judges, 'These solicitings cannot be evil, cannot be good.' Still, he is provided with so much natural good that he is able to control the apprehensions of his inordinate imagination and decides to take no step involving crime. His autonomous decision not to commit murder, however, is not in any sense based upon moral grounds. No doubt he normally shrinks from the unnaturalness of regicide; but he so far ignores ultimate ends that, if he could perform the deed and escape its consequences here upon this bank and shoal of time, he'ld jump the life to come. Without denying him still a complexity of motives—as kinsman and subject he may possibly experience some slight shade of unmixed loyalty to the King under his roof—we may even say that the consequences which he fears are not at all inward and spiritual. It is to be doubted whether he has ever so far considered the possible effects of crime and evil upon the human soul—his later discovery of horrible ravages produced by evil in his own spirit constitutes part of the tragedy. He is mainly concerned, as we might expect, with consequences involving the loss of mutable goods which he already possesses and values highly . . . .

[After the murder of Duncan the] natural good in him compels the acknowledgment that, in committing the unnatural act, he has filed his mind and has given his eternal jewel, the soul, into the possession of those demonic forces which are the enemy of mankind. He recognizes that the acts of conscience which torture him are really expressions of that outraged natural law, which inevitably reduces him as individual to the essentially human. This is the inescapable bond that keeps him pale, and this is the law of his own nature from whose exactions of devastating penalties he seeks release:

> Come, seeling night . . .
> And with thy bloody and invisible hand
> Cancel and tear to pieces that great bond
> Which keeps me pale.

He conceives that quick escape from the accusations of conscience may possibly be effected by utter extirpation of the precepts of natural law deposited in his nature. And he imagines that the execution of more bloody deeds will serve his purpose. Accordingly, then, in the interest of personal safety and in order to destroy the essential humanity in himself, he instigates the murder of Banquo . . . .

But he gains no satisfying peace because his conscience still obliges him to recognize the negative quality of evil and the barren results of wicked action. The individual who once prized mutable goods in the form of respect and admiration from those about him, now discovers that even such evanescent satisfactions are denied him:

> And that which should accompany old age,
> As honor, love, obedience, troops of friends,

I must not look to have; but, in their stead,
Curses, not loud but deep, mouth-honour, breath,
Which the poor heart.would fain deny, and dare not.

But the man is conscious of a profound abstraction of something far more precious than temporal goods. His being has shrunk to such little measure that he has lost his former sensitiveness to good and evil; he has supped so full with horrors and the disposition of evil is so fixed in him that nothing can start him. His conscience is numbed so that he escapes the domination of fears, and such a consummation may indeed be called a sort of peace. But it is not entirely what he expected or desires. Back of his tragic volitions is the ineradicable urge toward that supreme contentment which accompanies and rewards fully actuated being; the peace which he attains is psychologically a callousness to pain and spiritually a partial insensibility to the evidences of diminished being. His peace is the doubtful calm of utter negativity, where nothing matters . . . .

This spectacle of spiritual deterioration carried to the point of imminent dissolution arouses in us, however, a curious feeling of exaltation. For even after the external and internal forces of evil have done their worst, Macbeth remains essentially human and his conscience continues to witness the diminution of his being. That is to say, there is still left necessarily some natural good in him; sin cannot completely deprive him of his rational nature, which is the root of his inescapable inclination to virtue. We do not need Hecate to tell us that he is but a wayward son, spiteful and wrathful, who, as others do, loves for his own ends. This is apparent throughout the drama; he never sins because, like the Weird Sisters, he loves evil for its own sake; and whatever he does is inevitably in pursuance of some apparent good, even though that apparent good is only temporal or nothing more than escape from a present evil. At the end, in spite of shattered nerves and extreme distraction of mind, the individual passes out still adhering admirably to his code of personal courage, and the man's conscience still clearly admonishes that he has done evil . . . .

Moreover, he never quite loses completely the liberty of free choice, which is the supreme *bonum naturae* of mankind. But since a wholly free act is one in accordance with reason, in proportion as his reason is more and more blinded by inordinate apprehension of the imagination and passions of the sensitive appetite, his volitions become less and less free. And this accounts for our feeling, toward the end of the drama, that his actions are almost entirely determined and that some fatality is compelling him to his doom. This compulsion is in no sense from without—though theologians may at will interpret it so—as if some god, like Zeus in Greek tragedy, were dealing out punishment for the breaking of divine law. It is generated rather from within, and it is not merely a psychological phenomenon. Precepts of the natural law—imprints of the eternal law—deposited in his nature have been violated, irrational acts have established habits tending to further irrationality, and one of the penalties exacted is dire impairment of the liberty of free choice. Thus the Fate which broods over Macbeth may be identified with that disposition inherent in created things, in this case the fundamental motive principle of human action, by which providence knits all things in their proper order. Macbeth cannot escape entirely from his proper order; he must inevitably remain essentially human . . . .

. . . The substance of Macbeth's personality is that out of which tragic heroes are fashioned; it is endowed by the dramatist with an astonishing abundance and variety of potentialities. And it is upon the development of these potentialities that the artist lavishes the full energies of his creative powers. Under the influence of swiftly altering environment which continually furnishes or elicits new experiences and under the impact of passions constantly shifting and mounting in intensity, the dramatic individual grows, expands, develops to the point where, at the end of the drama, he looms upon the mind as a titanic personality infinitely richer than at the beginning. This dramatic personality in its manifold stages of actuation is an artistic creation. . . . In essence Macbeth, like all other men, is inevitably bound to his humanity; the reason of order, as we have seen, determines his inescapable relationship to the natural and eternal law, compels inclination toward his proper act and end but provides him with a will capable of free choice, and obliges his discernment of good and evil. . . .

Walter Clyde Curry

Macbeth, like *Richard III*, is best interpreted through its themes and imagery, not through 'character' (contrast *Othello*); and after a consideration of order, kingship and 'the state of man' in the Histories. . . .

. . . The outcome is a play about the distintegration of the state of man, and the state he makes his. It is commonly taken to be 'about ambition'; but ambition is only one of the names Macbeth finds for the impulsion in himself when looking into his own mind:

> I have no spur
> To prick the sides of my intent, but only
> Vaulting ambition, which o'erleaps itself. . . . (Act I, Sc. 7, 25-7);

and when he names it that, he rejects it: 'We will proceed no further. . . .' Better, I think, to call it 'particular will': a Shakespearian phrase for a force as much of the 'blood' as the intellect: Macbeth's *impulsion* (rather than his decision, as an ambitious man would feel it) to assert *his* pattern on the world: to make Macbeth Scotland. Instead, he finds he has made Scotland Macbeth: his damned soul has infected a whole country, even the whole universe. The forces *released* by the hope held in the Witches' prophecy; by the spurring of his wife, playing on his soldier's identification of honour (self-hood) with ruthless self-assertion through force: these give him the crown and sceptre. Both are hollow: the 'swelling prologue to the imperial theme' leads on to a *shrinking*, till 'there's nothing serious in mortality', and he becomes a tortured demon in a hell of his own begetting; glad of his own callousness; and (having half-conquered all), lord of nothing but chaos and the pitifully limited self-assertion of the will to fight until he drops.

A phrase of Coleridge's on the Weird Sisters states very well *what* it is that is released by Duncan's murder: 'they are the shadowy obscure and fearfully anomalous of physical nature, the lawless of human nature.' For Shakespeare, there is no compromise between order and chaos: the breakdown of ordered nature (in the mind, the state, the world) is absolute.

> Civilization is hooped together, brought
> Under a rule, under the semblance of peace
> By manifold illusion; (W.B. Yeats: *Supernatural Songs,* XII.)

or, rather, by one supreme illusion: a faith. But if that faith is once broken, then 'confusion' can 'make his masterpiece.' The very contemplation of the possibility of murdering the King brings the image and rhythm of confusion into Macbeth's mind:

> My thought, whose murder yet is but fantastical,
> Shakes so my single state of man
> That function is smother'd in surmise,
> And nothing is but what is not. (Act I, Sc. 3, 138-41)

This speech is exactly paralleled by Brutus's reflections before the murder of Caesar (*Julius Caesar*, Act II, Sc. 1, 60 ff.): he too refers to the state of man, like to a little kingdom, undergoing 'the nature of an insurrection'; and though he can provide himself with motives far more rational than Macbeth's, he also faintly recognizes the shadowy presence of the 'anomalous,' the fearful, the lawless and disordered, which his act ultimately releases. This parallelism of situation is emphasized by what are called 'the supernatural elements' in both plays. It would be more discriminating to call these elements 'sub-natural' or 'hypo-natural'; for they represent the irruption of forces *beneath* the normal order of integrated nature. In fact, they symbolize 'the horrifying old distrust of nature,' the dread of the unintelligible, the threat of the uncontrollable world with which 'humanity . . . is helplessly and irrevocably involved.' In Shakespeare's ethical symbolism, the macrocosmic universe, controlled by the unifying spirit of God, is imaged (I should prefer to say 'emblemed') in the State, controlled by the King seen as divine; and in the microcosm Man, whose ruling power holds in difficult subjection its lawless and passional undercurrents. It follows that the release of these mysterious and horrifying forces which strike at the illusion or faith that holds the State together as an organic whole, disturbs the complete order of all nature. The ultimate effect of Macbeth's 'horrible imaginings' at the very thought of breaking open 'the Lord's anointed temple,' is felt in Ross's lines to Lady Macduff:

> I dare not speak much further;
> But cruel are the times, when we are traitors

And do not know ourselves; when we hold rumour
From what we fear, yet know not what we fear,
But float upon a wild and violent sea
Each way and none. (Act IV, Sc. 2, 17-22)

They echo Macbeth's soliloquy-aside both in theme and in rhythm, ending with the same slip-away movement into sickening uncertainty. It is not merely that Macbeth's fears of the treachery he himself has taught have converted him into a cruel tyrant, so that no man knows where his safety ends, and fear reigns in all hearts—even of those who can tell themselves (vainly) that they should have nothing to fear. But that, with the release of the sub-human (or sub-natural), it is impossible for men even to know themselves, for good and evil (or virtue and vice) have lost their outlines. Men fear and do not know why, like brutes: but worse than brutes, in that they *know they do not know*, and experience the horror of the incomprehensible, the absolutely arbitrary: the thing that by all normal standards cannot be—yet is. It is this which gives what critics call the 'nightmare' quality to the play. It opens to the mind a vision of a world of men acting under hideous compulsions, in the unnatural wakefulness of 'murdered sleep.' This is easy to see in the case of Lady Macbeth; but Macbeth too speaks of 'the affliction of these terrible dreams/That shake us nightly', and envies Duncan his death:

Better be with the dead,
Whom we, to gain our peace, have sent to peace.
(Act III, Sc. 2, 19 ff.)

... [Macbeth, Lady Macbeth, and Banquo] are parts of a pattern, a design; are images, or symbols, and while a human being cannot simultaneously be full of the moral awareness of evil *and* fully engaged in doing it, wholly aware that the only motive he can offer himself is inadequate, those symbols we call *dramatis personae* not only *can* be, but must be, if the full weight and pressure of their acts are to be felt by the reader's or audience's minds. As Johnson put it, 'He has not only shewn human nature as it acts in real exigencies, but as it would be found in trials, to which it cannot be exposed'. In *Macbeth*, Shakespeare symbolizes the forces that operate in every moral conflict: and every deep conflict brings us to the contemplation of something powerful, anomalous and apparently ungraspable. I call that an impulsion, and use the name *will* for it for lack of a better: meaning thereby something less intellectual and consciously scheming, less argumentative, belonging more to the blood and the elementary passions, than we commonly think of when we use the term. It is the passionate will-to-self-assertion, to unlimited self-hood, and especially the impulsion to force the world (and everything in it) to *my* pattern, in *my* time, and with my own hand. Hence the reflection, 'If chance will have me King, why, chance may crown me,/Without my stir,' is powerless to restrain Macbeth. ...

Shakespeare presents this self-assertive force as a force promoting disorder, in man, in nature, in everything. The two 'protagonists' symbolize complementary aspects of its existence and operation. Neither is complete without the other. Before Duncan's murder, Lady Macbeth is the embodiment of this will, but it is not her 'woman's will' only: it is also a force of nature— ... There is an aspect of everything natural which tends towards concord, peace, trust and reliability (love): a natural order. There is also an aspect tending towards chaos, or complete and meaningless disorder (hate). 'Evil' is rather too definite a term for the second, though it is evil: the word tends to suggest a conscious Devil, bent on a definite plan of damnation, with 'ambition' as his bait. But Shakespeare's vision goes beyond this Christian simplification. On the human plane, he shows how the results of hard-willed self-assertion develop. First, to success; then to the ingrown insensibility of Macbeth as King, with his human sensitiveness either nulled or a hindrance; simultaneously, to the terrifying separateness of the damned, which both criminals endure; then to the remorseful harrassment of the night-wandering Queen; and finally to the state where Macbeth is merely monstrous, and outside him all are either enemies or tools or obstacles, in a world where 'everything includes itself in power,/Power into will, will into appetite', and humanity preys on itself 'like monsters of the deep.'

At this level, *Macbeth* is the tragedy of success. Macbeth becomes the embodiment of everything antagonistic and self-directed; and yet he is made the symbol of the utter emptiness of mere antagonism and self-assertion. The two contrary experiences—determination to force one's way on everything, ... and despair at the impossibility *and* the futility of doing so—are brought to co-existence in the mind. It is *in us* that Macbeth, his Lady and Banquo happen. They are not three persons, but one event in a poem. Murderers and Porter apart, all the rest of the *human* cast are antitheses to the two protagonists: often they have different names, but one essence or being.

A.P. Rossiter

If Macbeth's initial nobility, the manner of representation of his crimes, and his rich poetic gift are all calculated to sustain our sympathy, the kind of mistake he makes in initiating his own destruction is equally well suited to heighten our willingness to forgive while deploring. It could be said that he errs simply in being over-ambitious and under-scrupulous. But this is only part of the truth. What allows him to sacrifice his moral beliefs to his ambition is a mistake of another kind—a kind which is, at least to modern spectators, more credible than any conventional tragic flaw or any traditional tragic error, such as mistaking the identity of a brother or not knowing that one's wife is one's mother. Macbeth knows what he is doing, yet he does not know. He knows the immorality of the act, but he has no conception of the effects of the act on himself or his surroundings. Accustomed to heroic killing, in battle, and having valorously 'carv'd out his passage' with 'bloody execution' many times previously, he misunderstands what will be the effect on his own character if he tries to carve out his passage in civil life. And of course he cannot foresee that success in the first murder will only lead to the speech 'to be thus is nothing; But to be safely thus', and to ever increasing degradation and suffering for himself and for those around him. Even though he has a kind of double premonition of the effects of the deed both on his own conscience and on Duncan's subjects ('If it were done when 'tis done, then 'twere well ...'), he does not really understand. If he did understand, he could not, being who he is, do the deed.

This ignorance is made more convincing by being extended to a misunderstanding of the forces leading him to the murder. Macbeth does not really understand that he has two spurs, besides his own vaulting ambition, 'to prick the sides' of his intent. The first of these, the witches and their prophecy, might seem in no way to mitigate his responsibility, since he chooses wilfully to misinterpret what they say. But to reason in this way is again to overplay the role of logic in our dramatic experience. Surely the effect on the spectator is complex: while it is true that Macbeth ought to realize that if they are true oracles both parts of their prophecy must be fulfilled, it is also true that almost any man could be thrown off his moral balance by such supernatural confirmations. His misunderstanding is thus obvious and dramatically effective and at the same time quite forgivable.

The second force which Macbeth does not understand works less equivocally for our sympathy. While Lady Macbeth fills several functions in the play, beyond her great inherent interest as a character, her chief task, as the textbook commonplace has it, is to incite and confuse Macbeth—and thus ultimately to excuse him. ...

His tragic error, then, is at least three-fold: he does not understand the two forces working upon him from outside; he does not understand the difference between 'bloody execution' in civilian life and in military life; and he does not understand his own character—for he does not know what will be the effects of the act on his own future happiness .... The hero here must be really aware, in advance, of the wickedness of his act. The more aware he can be—and still commit the act convincingly—the greater the regret felt by the spectator.

All of these points are illustrated powerfully in the contrast between the final words of Malcolm concerning Macbeth—'This dead butcher and his fiend-like Queen'—and the spectator's own feelings toward Macbeth at the same point. We judge Macbeth, as Shakespeare intends, not merely for his actions but in the light of the total impression of the play. Malcolm and Macduff do not know Macbeth and the forces that have worked on him; the spectator does know him and can feel great pity that a man with so much potentiality for greatness should have fallen so low and should be so thoroughly misjudged. The pity is that everything was not otherwise, when it so easily could have been otherwise. The conclusion brings a flood of relief that the awful blunder has played itself out, that Macbeth has at least been able to die, still valiant, and is forced no longer to go on enduring the knowledge of what he has become.

Whether or not *Macbeth* may be considered in a sense 'topical' it contains elements that are, or might have been, mere theatrical entertainment. It combines with its great theme the working out of a puzzle, and affords us the pleasure of watching pieces dropping into place. That Macbeth would be king but no father of kings, that he would reign until Birnam Wood marched to Dunsinane, that he would be unconquerable by any man born of woman were riddling prophecies included in Holinshed, but the manner of presenting them through apparitions was Shakespeare's invention: the 'Armed Head' instigating the aggression against Macduff probably represents Macbeth himself; the 'Child Crowned with a tree in his hand' certainly represents young Malcolm, deviser of the tactics at Birnam Wood; the 'Bloody Child' represents Macduff, who was 'from his mother's womb Untimely ripped.' These ingenuities might well have been intrusive in a play so elemental; as handled by Shakespeare they contribute to the master plan by allowing us to watch Macbeth gradually stripped of hope by those 'juggling fiends' upon whom he has relied. . . .

. . . Whatever intrudes upon the stark simplicity of this work of art is an offense. It needs no help. Its brevity makes us wonder if there have been cuts as well as additions in the text printed in the folio, but it is hard to imagine any extension that would not have marred its present compact structure. The physical and spiritual terror rises in swift crescendos until Macduff's child is slaughtered at Fife and the universe seems riven in two, then comes the resting place of the scene in England like the still moment at the core of a hurricane; when the blast resumes, it is not to compound chaos but to orchestrate the restoration of moral order. No one who has read the play will ever forget the hardy characters who struggle to readmit light into their murky world, and certainly not that incandescent couple who kill together and die apart. The style has the vigor, condensation, and imaginative splendor of Shakespeare at his greatest, when he seems to be pressing upon the very bounds of the expressible. Blood and darkness are constantly invoked, and jarring antitheses, violent hyperbole, and chaotic imagery give the lines the quality demanded by the action. But there are also moments of unforgettable hush. Some of the speeches seem to express the agony of all mankind:

> Canst thou not minister to a mind diseased,
> Pluck from the memory a rooted sorrow,
> Raze out the written troubles of the brain,
> And with some sweet oblivious antidote
> Cleanse the stuffed bosom of that perilous stuff
> Which weighs upon the heart?

Over the centuries comes the quiet answer, convincing us, as so often the words of this poet so strangely do, that nothing further can be said,

> Therein the patient
> Must minister to himself.
>
> Alfred Harbage

Although the Bleeding Captain's report (Act I, Sc. 2) and the Drunken Porter scene (Act II, Sc. 3), as well as other passages, have been challenged as un-Shakespearian by various critics in the past, present-day opinion is almost unanimous in accepting them as Shakespeare's authentic creation. The only scenes now generally rejected as spurious are those in which Hecate appears: Act III, Sc. 5 (in its entirety) and Act IV, Sc. 1, 39-45 and 125-132.

There are several reasons for rejecting the Hecate passages. One is that the songs named to be sung by the Witches seem to have been composed by Thomas Middleton for his play *The Witch,* a tragicomedy that he composed three or four years after *Macbeth* was written (i.e., about 1609). Hecate also appears in *The Witch.* Evidently the Hecate scenes in *Macbeth* were inserted some years after Shakespeare composed his play; but it is most unlikely that he himself borrowed them. (It is supposed he retired from playwriting around 1611, a fact which further reduces the likelihood of his being instrumental in the matter.) But it does not follow that Middleton was responsible for inserting the Hecate passages in *Macbeth;* and in fact—because they do not resemble his style, either, apart from the identical titles of songs—the belief today is that he did not. We do not know who wrote the spurious passages.

Another reason for rejecting Hecate's own lines (apart from the songs) is that if Shakespeare had wanted the Queen of Hell to appear in this play, he would have introduced her in Act I, Sc. 1 or Act I, Sc. 3, not Act III, Sc. 5. And if he had done so, he assuredly would have given her a verse-rhythm and pattern of imagery resembling those with which he endows the Weird Sisters in the earlier scenes. On the contrary, Hecate's manner of expression contrasts obviously to that of the three Witches. Whereas they use the traditional trochaic, four-beat couplets long associated with supernatural beings and with incantations in drama—

> Round about the cauldron go;   [x]
>
> In the poison'd entrails throw—   [x]

Hecate speaks in iambic tetrameter couplets:

> And I, the mistress of your charms,
>
> The close contriver of all harms.

The Witches chant about gruesome or diabolical things. Hecate, however, uses but little imagery, and that is mostly conventional and prettified:

And now about the cauldron sing,
Like elves and fairies in a ring.

The tinkling, inane music of her lines contrasts to the harsh, menacing clusters of consonants and low vowels in the Witches' song:

Swelter'd venom sleeping got,
Boil thou first i'th'charmed pot.

In summary, no one today finds it credible that Shakespeare, for no apparent reason, should have so badly marred the tone of his witch scenes by the intrusion of Hecate, her attendants, and the songs borrowed from Middleton's play. But in order to amplify the spectacle of strange hags singing and dancing on stage, a feature that must have entranced the audience, someone was employed by the King's Men to make the additions to *Macbeth*, probably after Shakespeare's retirement.

G. R. Price

Review Questions and Answers

Question 1.
What do you understand by Dramatic Irony? Illustrate by reference to this play.

Answer
Most persons are familiar with the phrase, "The Irony of Fate." The expression has been handed down to us from the ancients, and suggests a pagan mode of thought. It is as if the gods were looking down in mockery upon human aspirations and human efforts, which they take pleasure in occasionally thwarting. The essence of Irony consists in double-dealing, whether in connection with action or with language. For the sake of illustration we will make a distinction between *Irony of Circumstance or Action* and *Irony of Language*.

IRONY OF CIRCUMSTANCE
This implies a sort of double-dealing in which Providence acts in a manner which is the reverse of what we might naturally expect. Such Dramatic Irony enters largely into the plot of *Macbeth*. The basis of Macbeth's rise is the promise given him by the witches that he shall be king hereafter. The promise is a mocking one; no sooner has it been uttered than an obstacle arises in the appointment of Malcolm as Prince of Cumberland and heir-apparent. This very obstacle, however, is the means of fixing Macbeth's wavering mind, and of leading him to undertake his treasonable enterprise. But there comes another obstacle. The king is slain, but his sons live, and it would seem that Macbeth's ambition is still unattainable. The flight of Malcolm and Donalbain, however, causes him to be named the

successor to the throne. Thus twice in the action of the play have obstacles been made to appear only in order to be used, with ironical effect, as an unexpected means of fulfilment.

Again, the witches' prophecy with regard to Macduff is an example of ironical action. Macbeth's security has only one obstacle—Macduff; and with the view of removing this obstacle he determines to destroy Macduff's whole family. His plan succeeds, except as regards Macduff himself. "This attempt against the fulfilment of the destined retribution (at the hands of Macduff) proves the very source of its fulfilment, without which it could never have come about. For at one point of the story Macduff, the only man who ... can harm Macbeth, resolves to abandon his vengeance against him." (R. G. Moulton, *Shakespeare As Dramatic Artist,* Oxford University Press, 1929) By the news of the massacre of his family Macduff's resolve is changed in a moment, and he exclaims—

> "Front to front
> Bring thou this fiend of Scotland and myself;
> Within my sword's length set him."　　　　(Act IV, Sc. 3, 225-7)

So that the very means which Macbeth adopted to rid himself of danger become by the irony of circumstances the very means by which he falls.

IRONY OF LANGUAGE

In this the *Dramatic Irony* lies in the fact that the audience knows what the actor does not know. The irony consists in ambiguous speech. The actor *seems* to speak ironically when in reality he is only expressing what he thinks to be absolutely true. A few examples will suffice to illustrate this form of irony.

(Act I, Sc. 4, 11)　　*Duncan:*　　　　　　"There's no art
To find the mind's construction in the face.
He was a gentleman on whom I built
An absolute trust"

spoken of the rebellious Cawdor immediately before the entrance of the still more faithless Macbeth. The irony consists in the fact that Duncan is again trusting one who is about to deceive him. Similarly in

(Act I, Sc. 4, 14)　　　　"O worthiest cousin!"

(Act I, Sc. 4, 56)　　　　"Let's after him,
Whose care is gone before to bid us welcome:
It is a peerless kinsman."

(Act I, Sc. 5, 38)　　*Lady Macbeth* to messenger:
"He brings great news."

| (Act I, Sc. 6) | The whole of this scene is full of the most subtle irony, *e.g.*, the "pleasant seat" of the castle, the "honour'd hostess," Macbeth's "great love, sharp as his spur," "we shall continue our graces towards him." |

(Act II, Sc. 3, 67)   *Macduff:*   "O gentle lady,
'Tis not for you to hear what I can speak:
The repetition, in a woman's ear,
Would murder as it fell."

(Act III, Sc. 4, 40)   *Macbeth:*
"Here had we now our country's honour roof'd,
Were the graced person of our Banquo present"

spoken at the moment of the entrance of Banquo's ghost.

Question 2.
Macbeth is a "tragedy of character rather than of deeds." Discuss.

Answer
Murder in itself is unfortunate, not tragic. The tragedy arises from the character responsible for, and to some extent from those characters affected by, the deeds. The tragedy in this play is classical (Aristotelian) in nature in that it is concerned with a great (and, up to a point, good) man whose noble qualities had won, and could have won him even more, "golden opinions" from all sorts of people, but who, because of fatal flaws in his nature (the craving for power, and the moral weakness that weakened his resistance to evil suggestions) took the wrong course, and was swept on to destruction, thus causing many lives to be wasted, and a whole nation brought to a state of anarchy. The realization that all his efforts had been in vain add bitterness to this tragedy. The spectacle of Macbeth's realization of how he had been duped by the supernatural equivocators belongs to the sphere of reflection on events, and the ability to reflect (after so long!) belongs to the sphere of character rather than of action. Therefore I would agree with the statement given in the question.

Question 3.
Point out the special purpose or purposes of soliloquies in Shakespeare's plays, illustrating your remarks by reference to this play.

Answer
The special purposes for which Shakespeare introduces soliloquies may be summarised as follows:—

(1) To illuminate and explain the characters of the more important persons.

108

(2) To supply details for the connection of the various links of the plot.

(3) To aid in keeping up the necessary unity by tracing the true sequence of cause and effect.

In Lady Macbeth's soliloquy on receiving the news of Duncan's coming visit we see how powerful must have been the motive which could compel her to do violence to her own woman's nature, causing her to summon to her aid the powers of darkness rather than forego her purpose. Nowhere, not even in her most confidential conversation with Macbeth does she so thoroughly unveil herself as in her soliloquies for in soliloquy there can be no concealment. With others there is always restraint, with ourselves none.

Macbeth, too, at the crucial moment, before he is forced into action, while yet all is uncertain and all depends on his decision, reveals himself in a soliloquy. In that in Act I, Sc. 3, "This supernatural soliciting," etc., we see the effect wrought on him by the witches' predictions, the temptation to which he is already succumbing. In Act I, Sc. 7, in the soliloquy "If it were done," etc., we again see him weighing one consideration with another. We see all his hesitation, his want of moral stability, his fear of the opinion of others, his sense of the insufficiency of his motive. Such feelings are carefully hidden in his conversations. He never reveals to his wife that he thinks the motive insufficient. Yet this fact is of importance to those who wish to understand his character.

Lady Macbeth's soliloquy in Act II, Sc. 2 elucidates the action of the play, and enables the spectators to imagine the events which are proceeding off the stage. "He is about it; the doors are open. ... I have drugged their possets. ... I laid their daggers ready; he could not miss 'em."

Banquo's soliloquy, which begins Act III, gives a glimpse of some of his characteristics. We see he was aware of Macbeth's guilt, that the powers of evil have secured some hold upon him, having awakened hopes, and that his inward struggle is undecided.

By means of soliloquy also scenes are described, as was necessary in an age when scenery was not used on the stage. Macbeth's speech, beginning "Now o'er the one half world. ..." (Act II, Sc. 1, 49-60) is highly descriptive, the speaker here performing the function of the author in a novel.

Question 4.
Discuss Shakespeare's use of (i) prose, (ii) rhymed verse, in *Macbeth*.

Answer
PROSE

Shakespeare usually employs prose (1) to produce a conversational effect, (2) in light or comic scenes, (3) for letters.

The principal prose passages in *Macbeth* are: (1) Macbeth's letter (Act I, Sc. 5); (2) the Porter's speech (Act II, Sc. 3); (3) part of Act IV, Sc. 2—Lady Macduff and her son; (4) the sleep-walking scene. The Porter's speech is the only approach to anything comic in the play. It serves to give relief to the intensity of the tragedy at this point.

In the conversation between Lady Macduff and her son, a light, chatty, natural effect is produced by the use of prose. So in the conversation in Act V, Sc. 1, between the Doctor and the Gentlewoman, prose is used as being compatible with the domestic surroundings. In this scene Lady Macbeth also speaks in prose, and the very simplicity of the style and diction renders the scene impressive.

RHYMED VERSE

Setting aside the Witches' parts, which are entirely in verse, we may say that Shakespeare uses rhyme in *Macbeth* for the following purposes:

(i) To close a scene, as in Act I, Sc. 7; Act V, Sc. 3.

(a)   "Away, and mock the time with fairest show,
               False face must hide what the false heart doth know."

(b)   "Were I from Dunsinane away and clear,
               Profit again should hardly draw me here."

(ii.) At the end of a speech to form an effective termination.

(a)   "Which shall to all our nights and days to come
               Give solely sovereign sway and masterdom."

                                      (Act I, Sc. 5, 69-70)

(b)   "The mind I sway by and the heart I bear
               Shall never sag with doubt nor shake with fear."

                                        (Act V, Sc. 3, 9-10)

By means of this device attention was directed to the close of the scene. This was important in the days when plays were performed without change of scenery or dropping of curtains.

(iii.) Again, the close of a scene or speech is frequently epigrammatic, or it contains a summary of the situation. Rhyme in this case ensured the noticing of the point by the audience.

(a)   "It is concluded. Banquo, thy soul's flight,
               If it find heaven, must find it out to-night."

                                      (Act III, Sc. 1, 140-1)

(b)   "Thou marvell'st at my words: but hold thee still,
               Things bad begun make strong themselves by ill."

                                      (Act III, Sc. 2, 54-5)

(iv.) Anything of the nature of a maxim or proverbial saying is usually expressed in rhyme.

(a)   "Come what come may,
Time and the hour runs through the roughest day."
(Act I, Sc. 3, 146-7)

(b)   "Give sorrow words: the grief that does not speak
Whispers the o'erfraught heart and bids it break."
(Act IV, Sc. 3, 202-3)

(v) It marks the first resolve of a mind made up, in
"Blow, wind! come, wrack!
At least we'll die with harness on our back."
(Act V, Sc. 5, 51-2
and Act V, Sc. 8, 33-4.)

(vi.) It indicates an "aside," not otherwise clearly marked in
"The Prince of Cumberland! that is a step
On which I must fall down, or else o'erleap," etc.
(Act I, Sc. 4, 48-53)

(vii.) In making the Witches speak in rhyme Shakespeare followed his usual custom with regard to supernatural beings (*cf.* the fairies in *A Midsummer Night's Dream*). In this case the metre used is trochaic, as suiting their rapid utterance. Hecate speaks in iambic rhyme. This fact, together with a certain un-Shakespearian quality perceptible in her verses, has caused it to be doubted whether the lines were written by Shakespeare at all.

Question 5.
Illustrate from the play Macbeth's openness, ambition, strong imagination.

Answer
MACBETH'S OPENNESS

The whole tendency of Macbeth's nature is to be open and straightforward. His courage prompts him always to take the shortest way to his end. In the battle, "like valour's minion [he] carved out his passage till he faced the slave," and so he would have done throughout the battle of life had not circumstances and his ambition been too strong for him. Yet even when most he needed hypocrisy he proved to be a poor dissembler. His face "is as a book where men may read strange matters." "What he would highly, that would he holily," says his wife, who knew him well. Honesty prevails with him at least so far that once he has entertained thoughts of murdering Duncan he cannot bear to be near him. He escapes the necessity of being the king's harbinger to Inverness. Again, fearing lest he should betray himself, he escapes from the presence of the king at supper (Act I, Sc. 7), because he cannot bear to receive his praises and to see his satisfaction. In the smallest trifles his instinctive truthfulness is apparent. Lennox asks, "Goes the king hence to-day?" "He does," says Macbeth, but immediately after modifies his statement, saying "he did appoint so." (Act II, Sc. 3, 37) He experiences the greatest difficulty in concealing from his wife his intentions with regard to Banquo, and confesses to her the torture of his mind, which he would fain have kept to himself, but could not.

HIS AMBITION

In Macbeth's ambition we find the keynote to his character. It supplies the motive force to almost all his actions of the first half of the play. That the evil suggestions of the witches find a responsive chord in his mind is evident from the guilty "start" which he made at his first interview with them, and from the eagerness with which he demands to know more. Lady Macbeth, in her analysis of his character, refers to his ambition, whilst he himself confesses that his only incentive to the murder of Duncan is:

> "Vaulting ambition, which o'erleaps itself
> And falls on the other."

For the sake of his ambition he silences his conscience and the voice of honour, he disregards the dues of loyalty and of hospitality, and after having committed one murder he wades through blood to others, all through fear of having possessed himself of a "barren sceptre" only.

HIS STRONG IMAGINATION

Macbeth is highly imaginative and impressionable. He hears voices and sees visions imperceptible by the senses of others. The supernatural attracts him, and the unreal is to him more real than the actual facts. "Present fears are less than horrible imaginings ... and nothing is but what is not." To his imagination we owe many of the finest passages of the play. We may note particularly the passages Act II, Sc. 1, 49-60, Act II, Sc. 2, 34-42, Act II, Sc. 3, 93-9, and Act III, Sc. 2, 46-55. His imagination was, at the same time, a source of his strength and his weakness. At one moment it pictures to him the air-drawn dagger leading him to Duncan, at another it presents to him the considerations which should restrain him. (Act I, Sc. 7, 1-28) Finally, it is his imagination which forces him to think that "Returning were as tedious as go o'er," and contributes to make of him a desperate man, regardless of crime.

Question 6.

Discuss the influence of the witches' prophecies on Macbeth's decision to murder Duncan.

Answer

Central to the subject at hand must be the understanding that the witches do not make Macbeth do anything. All they do is greet Macbeth as the Thane of Glamis, as the Thane of Cawdor, and as the future king.

These are merely greetings, and because Macbeth does not know that he is either the Thane of Cawdor or the king, Macbeth, Banquo, and the audience take the greetings as prophecies. But a prophecy is not an invitation to murder. Nor is it even a suggestion that one is aggressively to seek out the office predicted for one. But that is exactly how Macbeth takes the prophecies. He calls them "supernatural soliciting," an invitation to seek the kingship. However, Macbeth has had murder on his mind as a method of gaining the kingship, and in effect he therefore takes the predictions as a beckoning by supernatural powers to murder Duncan for the kingship.

But both the audience and Macbeth have been warned that the witches are dangerous and that their remarks must be carefully not carelessly construed. Banquo, just after Macbeth has been told of his creation as Thane of Cawdor and just before Macbeth calls the prophecies "supernatural soliciting," warns Macbeth that often "The instruments of darkness tell us truth; / Win us with honest trifles, to betray's / In deepest consequence." In effect Banquo is telling Macbeth not to be led astray by the fact that one of the predictions has come true. The witches may be instruments of the devil, and everyone knows that no one must do what the devil tells him to do. This is made obvious at the beginning of this very scene. We may remember that the first witch wishes to punish a sailor's wife because the latter did not give her some chestnuts, which she wanted. She will punish the wife, whose husband is the captain of the *Tiger*, by tossing his ship about in the wind and causing him sleeplessness. He "Shall dwindle, peak, and pine: / Though his bark cannot be lost, / Yet it shall be tempest tost." What applies to the captain also applies to Macbeth. The first witch, as an instrument of the devil, can toss about the *Tiger*, but she cannot cause its sinking. So with Macbeth: the witches may cause Macbeth all kinds of painful temptations; they may toss about his bark (a common Renaissance metaphor for soul), but they cannot cause it to sink. Only Macbeth, by succumbing to temptation, can do that.

Now, although the witches did not cause Macbeth to murder Duncan, they did provide temptation. We cannot tell whether or not Macbeth would have murdered Duncan without the seeming guarantee of success that the witches offered. But that they made it easier for Macbeth to succumb to his wife; that they made Lady Macbeth more determined to whip her husband into committing the crime, we can have little doubt. The devil was out to get Macbeth because he knew that Macbeth was open to temptation, but the devil had to be careful in giving temptation its most pleasing form: in essence, flattery. That is the "charm" the witches wind up, not the charm which forces Macbeth into murder.

We may conclude, therefore, that the witches are part of this deceptive, treacherous world, which can offer great temptation, but which cannot make us fall for the temptation if we are strong enough.

Question 7.

Trace the course in the play of the relationship of Macbeth and Lady Macbeth.

Answer

When the play begins, the relationship between the two leading characters is almost an ideal relationship between a man and a wife. They love each other deeply, and they are on the most intimate terms mentally and emotionally. This is clear early in the play. Almost as soon as Macbeth heard the witches' prophecies, he wrote to his wife about them, certainly an indication of intimacy. Then, in the letter he says, "This [the news of his meeting with the witches] have I thought good to deliver thee, my dearest partner of greatness, that though might'st not lose the dues of rejoicing, by being ignorant of what greatness is promised thee." We may notice that Macbeth calls his wife his "dearest partner of greatness." He thinks of her as sharing the throne with him, an indication this time not only of intimacy but also of love. He also talks of "what greatness is promised thee," almost as though his becoming king is important only in so far as it will bring her greatness. But his feeling for her is shared by her for him. Just as he talks of "what greatness is promised thee," so she in talking of the crown never refers to it, in the speech in which she reads the letter, as a goal to be attained by her or by both of them but rather only by Macbeth. It is as though she were doing this only for him and not at all for herself.

However, we must not overlook another component in her relationship to Macbeth. She feels that her husband "is too full o' the milk of human kindness, / To catch the nearest way." Therefore, she will "chastise with the valor of my tongue / All that impedes [Macbeth] from the golden round." As it turns out, Macbeth is reluctant to commit the murder of Duncan, and his wife shames him into doing it. Of course, she can not believe her own accusations of cowardice; she is using what she knows will mobilize him. Nor does she argue his points. She is, in effect, manipulating him. True, she is manipulating him for what she considers his own good, but manipulation nevertheless it is. We must say, then, that in Lady Macbeth's love for her husband there is that which says, "I know better what is good for him than he does himself, and I will force him to it whether he currently likes it or not." Any love which says that has a component of egotism influencing it. Nevertheless, the love and the sense of intimacy on both sides is strong.

As the relationship in the play proceeds, one of the play's ironies is developed. Namely, in part because of their great love, Macbeth and his wife become increasingly separated from each other. Certainly they become separated also because Macbeth becomes more and more desperate as his wife increasingly falls under the sway of her conscience. But, as we implied, even more interesting is their separation caused by their love. Macbeth knows that his wife is tortured by the murder of

Duncan. Therefore, to prevent further guilt, he does not tell her of his arrangement to murder Banquo, and apparently more and more he acts for himself. Of course, once she has withdrawn into herself, their separation becomes greater, and with her death their separation becomes permanent. Because of the evil with which they were involved, even their love, fine as it was, could not last.

Question 8.

Illustrate by quotations from the play, and explain, as far as possible, Macbeth's deterioration in character.

Answer

When first we hear of Macbeth there is clearly much in him worthy of admiration. He is courageous. "He is skilful in war. He is a leader whom men gladly follow; and how much nobility of disposition does that one fact imply!" But his good qualities do not amount to *character*. Weak men have wishes, strong men have wills. Macbeth's tendencies to what is good, amount to little more than a wish to be good, and to stand well with his fellows.

In the opening scenes of the play we witness a struggle between Macbeth's conscience and his evil instincts. Evil gains the mastery, and so gives the tragic tone to the whole of the play. At first Macbeth is unwilling to commit so vile a deed

> "Whose horrid image doth unfix my hair
> And make my seated heart knock at my ribs,
> Against the use of nature."   (Act I, Sc. 3, 135)

He is not yet in alliance with crime, he is neutral. He might by an effort yet overcome the promptings of his evil ambition. But he cannot make the effort, and another influence is at work on the side of evil. With his characteristic openness he has made his wife acquainted with his secret thoughts. She, knowing his desires, will not allow of any hesitation. Macbeth has said—

> "If chance will have me king, why chance may crown me
> Without my stir."   (Act I, Sc. 3, 144)

but Lady Macbeth will have him pursue a more direct and rapid path to the summit of his ambition. Still he essays to discard the topic, and to put her off with "We will speak further" (Act I, Sc. 5, 70). Again for a moment his good instincts triumph over his evil desires: "We will proceed no further in this business," he says (Act I, Sc. 7, 31). Once more the strenuous energy of his wife combines with the ever-present suggestion of a guilty ambition to overcome his hesitation. His fall is now assured. "I am settled," he says, "and bend up

"Each corporal agent to this terrible feat."   (Act I, Sc. 7, 80)

He thought the murder of Duncan would be the "Sesame to Royalty." But the assassination could not "trammel up the consequences." On the contrary, this deed was but the living seed from which all his later crimes were to spring. It was the first stepping stone in the long series which led him on from that one fatal night to the final tragedy of his own death. "Repentance immediately follows, nay, even precedes the deed, and the stings of his conscience leave him no rest either night or day. But he is now fairly entangled in the snares of hell" (Schlegel). A second murder follows the first, and in the bitterness and despair of his own self-abasement he declares,

> "I am in blood,
> Stepp'd in so far, that should I wade no more
> Returning were as tedious as go o'er."   (Act III, Sc. 4, 138)

There is now no expression of remorse. He knows that he is being dragged downwards, and the knowledge only hurries him on to his ruin.

> "For Banquo's issue have I fil'd my mind,"

he says, and he who had before confided in fate now challenges it.

> "Rather than so, come, fate, into the list,
> And champion me to the utterance.   (Act III, Sc. 1, 70)

All scruples are set aside, and he resolves to seek out the weird sisters who before had sought him out.

> "More shall they speak, for now I am bent to know,
> By the worst means the worst."   (Act III, Sc. 4, 135)

It is no obstacle to him now that he knows they are spirits of evil, for his mind is made up

> "For mine own good
> All causes shall give way."   (Act III, Sc. 4, 136)

"He is an unconscious fury rushing towards evil. The first step taken, the fatal descent begins. He falls and rebounds from one crime to another always lower"—(Victor Hugo).

His deterioration in character was due, as we have seen, to his weakness in the face of temptation, to the promptings of an evil ambition and the influence of his wife. For a time he struggled against evil. His struggles became weaker with each victory that temptation won over him, until finally he became the willing slave of evil, in whom the higher voice of nature was dead. Of his cruelties one specimen is afforded by the murder of Macduff's family, of his inward desolation we are convinced by the manner in which he received the news of his wife's death, and his subsequent speech, commencing—

"To-morrow, and to-morrow, and to-morrow."

Question 9.

Sketch the character of Banquo, paying particular attention to his connection with the witches.

Answer

THE CHARACTER OF BANQUO

Forms a companion picture to that of Macbeth. In courage, energy, and service to the public weal he resembles Macbeth. Like Macbeth also he possesses a character which appears to be only partially developed. He is honourable, generous, modest, with a preference for what is good over what is not good, yet he never actively exerts himself to set wrong right, and even when his duty lay clear before him he hesitated so long that death overtook him before he had definitely made up his mind to act. He differs from Macbeth in two important respects—in his lack of ambition for himself, and in his power of prayer. Hence, under him, Macbeth's "Genius is rebuked," for "In his royalty of nature reigns that which would be fear'd."

HIS ATTITUDE TOWARDS THE WITCHES

Is at first merely that of an enquirer. He betrays no unnatural curiosity at the interview. "Speak to me who neither beg nor fear your favours nor your hate." He has not been entertaining secret ambitions as Macbeth has, and therefore the witches' intimations meet with no responsive chord to set his whole nature thrilling. Nevertheless he is powerfully affected by their utterances, as Macbeth was. But he recognises them as the "instruments of darkness" which "tell us truths" to "win us to our harms." Consequently he resolutely struggles against the suggestions that they have implanted in his mind. How difficult he found the struggle is evident from his words—

> "Merciful powers
> Restrain in me the cursed thoughts that nature
> Gives way to in repose."   Act II, Sc. 1, 7-9

He knows that they cannot force him to evil in spite of himself, and he does his utmost to stifle the ambitious thoughts which they have stirred within him. But he should have done more than this. Knowing that Macbeth was a traitor and a murderer, it was his duty to his country to denounce him; it was his duty to himself to be on his guard against him. Being remiss in both these duties he helped to bring about his country's ruin and his own destruction.

Question 10.

Quote allusions to (i) Night, (ii) Sleep, (iii) Dreams, and show their importance in connection with the play.

Answer
NIGHT

Has always been regarded as the special season of crime when "such bitter business" is done "as the day would quake to look on." At such a time

> "Good things of day begin to droop and drowse;
> While night's black agents to their preys do rouse."
> (Act III, Sc. 2, 52-3)

It was at night that the powers of evil were supposed to possess the greatest influence and resistance to temptation to be weakest. Lady Macbeth calls on Night to envelop their murderous deeds lest "Heaven peep through the blanket of the dark to cry 'Hold, hold!' " (Act I, Sc. 5, 52). Macbeth plans the murder of Banquo to take place at night

> "Ere the bat hath flown
> His cloister'd flight," etc.
> (Act III, Sc. 2, 40-4)

The night of Duncan's murder was "unruly," and was prolonged unnaturally.

> "By the clock 'tis day,
> And yet dark night strangles the travelling lamp."
> (Act II, Sc. 4, 6)

Hecate spends the night before Macbeth's second interview with the witches in preparing to lure him on to his ruin. "This night I'll spend unto a dismal and a fatal end" (Act III, Sc. 5, 20).

SLEEP

Was the emblem of peace; peace of body, mind, and soul. No wonder, then, that Macbeth felt in murdering Duncan that he had murdered his own peace of soul and forfeited the priceless boon of sleep: "Methought I heard a voice cry 'Sleep no more,' Macbeth doth murder sleep," etc. (Act II, Sc. 2, 35-43). Even Lady Macbeth is profoundly affected by the sight of "innocent sleep." She would, she says, have murdered Duncan with her own hands "Had he not resembled my father as he slept." Macbeth's account of the grooms praying in their sleep moves her deeply (Act II, Sc. 2, 33). And it is a remarkable fact that as her contact with sleep was the means of deterring her from committing murder, sleep itself was the means by which she betrayed her guilt. Banquo recognises the weakness of the will under the influence of sleep (Act II, Sc. 1, 7-8); whilst Lady Macbeth testifies to its value as "tired Nature's sweet restorer" when she says to her husband, "You lack the season of all nature's sleep." From earliest times the comparison between sleep and death has been dwelt upon by poets. Lady Macbeth says "the sleeping and the dead are but as pictures" (Act II, Sc. 2, 52). Macduff speaks of sleep as "death's counterfeit," and Macbeth says of Duncan, almost enviously, "After life's fitful fever he sleeps well" (Act III, Sc. 2, 23).

DREAMS

The different allusions to dreams bear out the strain of the supernatural which runs through the play, and determines the course of the action. Banquo's temptation comes to him in dreams—"I dreamt last night of the three weird sisters" (Act II, Sc. 1, 20); "Merciful powers, restrain in me the cursed thoughts that nature gives way to in repose" (Act II, Sc. 1, 7). From these and other allusions dreams seem to be looked upon as one of the agencies of evil. Macbeth speaks of "wicked dreams" which "abuse the curtained sleep." They are sent also as punishments to the guilty. Macbeth sleeps "in the affliction of these terrible dreams that shake us nightly."

Bibliography

A. C. Bradley, *Shakespearean Tragedy* (New York: World Publishing Company, 1961). First Published in 1904, this is a classic of Shakespearean criticism, lucid and profound. *Macbeth* chapters deal with characters and atmosphere.

Lily B. Campbell, *Shakespeare's Tragic Heroes, Slaves of Passion* (New York: Barnes and Noble, 1961). The heroes of the great tragedies in the light of Elizabethan psychology. Macbeth wavers between fear and rashness.

Thomas De Quincey, "On the Knocking at the Gate in *Macbeth.*" *Shakespeare Criticism, 1623-1840,* ed. D. Nichol Smith (London: Oxford University Press, 1961). Classic of romantic criticism.

Francis Fergusson, "*Macbeth* as the Imitation of an Action," *English Institute Essays* (New York: Columbia University Press, 1952). The governing idea is the violation of nature.

T. Hawkes, *Twentieth Century Interpretations of Macbeth,* (Englewood Cliffs, N.J.: Prentice-Hall, 1977), A collection of critical essays.

G. Wilson Knight, *The Imperial Theme* (London: Methuen, 1951). Work of an influential symbolist critic. Contains essay on "life-themes" in *Macbeth*.

Kenneth Muir, ed., *Macbeth* (New York: Random House ["New Arden" edition, paperback], 1962). Most substantial edition of the play. Contains useful introduction that, among other things, gives survey of nineteenth-century *Macbeth* criticism.

———, ed., *Shakespeare Survey,* Vol. XIX (Cambridge: Cambridge University Press, 1966). Volume devoted to *Macbeth.* Contains significant studies and useful review of twentieth-century *Macbeth* criticism.

John Middleton Murry, *Shakespeare* (New York: Harcourt, Brace, 1936). Neo-romantic criticism of dramas. Imagery of time in *Macbeth*.

Irving Ribner, *Patterns in Shakespearean Tragedy* (London: Methuen, 1960). *Macbeth* and other tragedies in relation to Shakespeare's inherited ideas and dramatic forms.

M. Rosenberg, *The Masks of Macbeth* (Berkeley: University of California Press, 1978). Good analysis of characterization.

L. L. Shücking, *Character Problems in Shakespeare's Plays* (New York: Holt, 1922). Dramatic conventions in characterization. Macbeth essentially ignoble.

Paul N. Siegel, *Shakespearean Tragedy and the Elizabethan Compromise* (New York: New York University Press, 1957). Shakespearean tragedy in relation to contemporary social and intellectual changes. Two opposing views of manhood in *Macbeth*.

Caroline F.E. Spurgeon, *Shakespeare's Imagery and What it Tells Us* (New York: Cambridge University Press, 1935).

E. M. W. Tillyard, *Shakespeare's History Plays* (New York: Macmillan Company, 1946). *Macbeth* in relation to the history plays and Elizabethan political thought.

D. A. Traversi, *Approach to Shakespeare* (London: Sands, 1957). Close analysis of language and verse of dramas. "Degree" in *Macbeth*.

Mark Van Doren, *Shakespeare* (New York: Holt, 1939). Brief, perceptive essays. Time and atmosphere in *Macbeth*.

Roy Walker, *The Time is Free* (London: Dakers, 1949). Book-length study of *Macbeth*. Imagery, irony, and the tragic pattern.

NOTES